SECRET SISTER

FROM NAZI-OCCUPIED JERSEY TO WARTIME LONDON, ONE WOMAN'S SEARCH FOR THE TRUTH

CHERRY DURBIN

WITH GILL PAUL

HarperElement
An imprint of HarperCollins*Publishers*
1 London Bridge Street
London SE1 9GF

www.harpercollins.co.uk

First published by HarperElement 2015

13 5 7 9 10 8 6 4 2

© Cherry Durbin 2015

Long Lost Family is produced in the UK
by Wall to Wall Media Ltd

Cherry Durbin asserts the moral right to
be identified as the author of this work

A catalogue record of this book is
available from the British Library

ISBN 978-0-00-813307-8

Printed and bound in Great Britain by
Clays Ltd, St Ives plc

MIX
Paper from
responsible sources

FSC
www.fsc.org

FSC™ C007454

For John, my Essex boy, my soulmate, who accepted me as I was and didn't try to change me. I carry you in my heart into this new phase of my life.

For Mum and Pop, who gave me love and stability for the first eight years to build the rest of my life on.

And for my kids, Helen and Graham, who've had to put up with me since they were born. I love you and I'm so proud of you.

Foreword by
Davina McCall

Long Lost Family has been the most rewarding, warm and moving programme I have had the honour to work on.

Helping someone to find a missing relative can bring answers to questions that go to the very depths of their identity. Where do I come from? Who am I? Why was I given up for adoption? Why do I look like this? What's the family medical history? The answers can bring great joy, but they might also be horribly distressing, so it was crucial that I, and everyone else on the *Long Lost Family* team, treated everyone on the programme with the utmost care and sensitivity. I always love it when the people who share their stories with us tell me what a fantastic journey it's been. Our production team are *amaaaaaaaaaaaaaaaazing* and on location we want everyone to feel special …

I have been open about the fact that I had a difficult relationship with my own mother – a wonderful, wild woman who just wasn't cut out to be motherly. My first memory is of her taking me to my grandparents' and telling me she was going on holiday and that she'd be back in two weeks. She never came back. I saw her in the holidays, which were always pretty chaotic … I was often forgotten or just exposed to stuff I shouldn't have been. I always relate to people on the show who have been left by their mothers. I understand now how hard it must have been for my mother – as an adult I have more sympathy – but I have lived with the effects of her actions for my entire life. In some ways they have made me stronger, but in other ways …

Deep down, people looking for missing family members are hoping for some kind of closure to a mystery at the very heart of their lives. My wonderful cousin Claire was adopted and she found us twelve years ago – she was looking for her mother. She found her and an enormous clan! I am so, so pleased to have her and her son in our lives.

No matter what the future holds, the answers we find for the people on the show are all-important. They are bound to feel very exposed. I have a special responsibility as the person delivering the news that might change their lives for ever. And if Nicky or I go to talk to the missing family member, that's an equally sensitive job. They might feel guilty about decisions they made decades before, they may be scared of rejection – and they are often scared. From reading the first few stories we were sent, and seeing the honesty with which they were written, I knew I was going to get massively emotionally involved, but that I would also have to keep a lid on my feelings. This show isn't about me; it's about the families.

When I first heard Cherry Durbin's story, I was struck by the fact that she had been lonely for a lot of her life: she'd been brought up as an only child, had particularly lonely teenage years, a lonely first marriage, and now, in her late sixties, she was living alone. Yet, tantalisingly, she knew she had a big sister called Sheila who was out there somewhere, hopefully still alive. She'd been searching for Sheila for almost three decades and had made a little bit of headway, but every time she got her hopes up she was met with a dead end. There was a fascinating story to be told about the German occupation of the Channel Islands during the Second World War and the way it split up families, with some evacuated while others stayed behind. We knew we wanted to take on Cherry's story simply because it was obvious how much it would mean to her if we could find Sheila.

When Cherry and I met, I liked her immediately, but her loneliness was etched on her face ... a sort of deep sadness. She was sweet and vulnerable, and yet strong.

And I was curious about her stoicism. 'No matter what happens, I won't cry,' she said. 'I'm not the crying type.' She told me she had learned to keep her emotions compartmentalised from an early age, and I wondered how she would cope with what I had to tell her. I'm not going to give away the ending – you'll have to read Cherry's story to find out about the incredible news I was able to give her – but true to her word, she didn't break down and sob. If you watch the show, though, I think you'll see the glint of tears in her eyes, as well as utter astonishment.

When family reunions take place I'm usually hiding behind a door/pillar/potted plant, sobbing with Nicky, well out of shot, so I don't see what happens until I'm back at home, watching from my sofa with a box of tissues to hand. Nicky Campbell has often telephoned to tell me a little about the missing relatives he has met, but if I don't get to meet them first, I love to watch how each reunion unfolds.

I'm sure Cherry was prepared for disappointment, because she'd been disappointed so many times before, and I genuinely couldn't be more pleased about the way things have turned out for her. In this book, you'll read her story in her own words, and I think you'll get a sense of what a strong, positive, lovely woman she is. It was a great privilege to be with her on the day she learned the truth about her birth family, an event that I know has changed her life significantly.

I had no idea when I started presenting *Long Lost Family* back in 2011 that it would run to a fifth series, but here we are in 2015 with yet another set of moving stories to share. I'm over the moon that the show has been so well received, and I was totally overwhelmed when we won the BAFTA award for best feature in 2014, because we were up against extremely strong competition. *Long Lost Family* seems to strike a chord with all kinds of people, from all walks of life, whether or not they have missing family members or difficult backgrounds of their own. There's something universal about the emotions involved – love and fear, guilt and forgiveness – that we can all identify with.

As time went on, I wondered if I would stop getting emotionally involved in each and every story, but it hasn't happened yet. I still find myself welling up when I hear we've got good news for someone, or having a weep in the car outside if a story strikes a personal chord. But after filming, I'll go home and give my kids an extra-tight bedtime hug, because I realise how lucky I am to have them and my fantastic husband Matthew by my side.

My thanks to everyone on the *Long Lost Family* team (I really, really love you guys … you are the very best at what you do), and to all of you out there who watch the

show, and especially to those who have the courage to
share your extraordinary stories with us – I take my hat off
to you!

Big Hugs x

Prologue

One evening in May 2011, I was slumped on the sofa with my collies, Bear and Max, beside me, half-reading a book and half-dozing. It had been a long, busy day. I'm a very early riser because I've got two horses, Kali and Raz, in a stable down the road and they need to be rubbed down, mucked out, fed and taken to their field at the crack of dawn. Horses don't like to hang around waiting while humans have a lie-in, so that's the first thing I do in the morning, come rain, snow, hail or sunshine. Next there are the dogs to walk, and they're big, energetic dogs who like a good, long run around. I help out at the local kennels and in exchange they let me leave Bear and Max with them if I have to go away somewhere. And I also pop in to look after some elderly folks in the area, including one lady with dementia. So for a 68-year-old I had a pretty full life. It did mean I wasn't fit for much come the evening (by which time I'd got the horses and dogs back indoors, rubbed down, fed and so forth).

I don't really watch much telly, but it's sometimes turned on as background noise, just as company really because I live alone now. My set is only a tiny, portable one that I got third-hand from my daughter Helen, so it's easy to ignore, but that evening I suddenly remembered that *Long Lost Family* was on. I found the show fascinating because I had been searching for my own family for almost thirty years and knew what a difficult emotional journey it could be. I'd missed the beginning of the programme but on the screen a pretty, dark-haired woman was talking about her search for the mother who'd given her up for adoption back in the sixties.

'I had a really happy childhood with my adoptive family,' she said. 'It's just that I've always felt different from them. They don't look like me … I want there to be someone out there who looks a bit like me, who *is* a bit like me.'

Now, I knew that feeling of not entirely fitting in because I had been adopted by parents who didn't particularly look like me, with whom I didn't share any genetic features. Mum and Pop were a wonderful couple and I'd loved them to pieces, but both had passed away long ago.

On screen, the girl was saying she was anxious that if they tracked down her birth mother, the woman might not want to know her. I could identify with her anxiety because I'd been in that exact same situation. The more I'd probed into my own past, the more I'd hit brick walls and dead ends. I'd had some success – just enough to find out that I had a sister, Sheila, somewhere, but I had no idea where. I was determined to find her one day because I needed answers to all kinds of mysteries from my past, things that simply didn't add up. I was a widow, with two wonderful children and four grandchildren of my own, but I had no family roots, no one of my generation or older to help me understand where I came from and to make me feel there was a family I belonged to. Basically, I was lonely, and I'd been lonely for much of my life since Mum had died. I'd been a lonely teenager, I'd had a lonely and difficult first marriage, and now at the age of sixty-eight I was on my own again.

On screen the presenter, Davina McCall, told the girl that they had finally found her birth mother, and I found my eyes filling with tears. It was odd, because I'm not the crying type. I'm so well practised at bottling up my emotions that they rarely see the light of day. I suppose this girl's story touched a nerve for me because it was so close to my own.

The girl and her birth mother met in a park and gave each other a huge hug. The mum was murmuring, 'Thank you, thank you,' and I could tell they were both lovely, friendly people. They seemed very similar, and you could definitely see a family likeness. I hoped it would work out for them and that they'd find what they were looking for in each other.

The team did two searches in each programme and they succeeded in reuniting the family members in the other story as well. They always did. I'd run out of ideas, having tried everything I could possibly think of to find my missing sister.

And then at the end of the programme there was an announcement: 'If you have a long-lost family member and would like to take part in the next series of *Long Lost Family*, please email us at this address.' I grabbed a piece of paper and a pen and scribbled it down. Fortunately, I always have paper and a pen lying around to write notes to remind myself of things I would otherwise forget.

I picked up the phone and rang my daughter Helen. 'Were you just watching telly?' I asked. She was, but a different programme, so I explained to her what I'd seen.

'That's funny!' Helen said. 'You were telling me just the other day that you must do something about finding Sheila. It's as if this is a sign.'

I felt the same way myself. 'Will you email them for me?' I asked. I had a computer but it hadn't been working for ages and I felt no pressing need to get it fixed. I was more of an outdoorsy person than a desk type. 'You know all about my story.'

'OK, Mum. I'll do it tomorrow. Wouldn't it be amazing if they could find Sheila? I'd have a new auntie!'

'Oh, I don't think they will,' I said. 'It's all too late and too long ago. But it would be interesting to let them try. They might have methods I haven't thought of ...'

'Yeah, like using the internet,' Helen said with a sarcastic edge to her voice.

'You never know. I'll call you tomorrow, Nell.'

As I got into bed, I couldn't help picturing myself on the programme at that moment when you meet your family member against a beautiful backdrop. It would be so wonderful if they found Sheila. I'd always wanted a sibling, and I'd been searching for her for almost thirty years now. It nagged away at me, something I couldn't let go of, a piece of unfinished business.

But then I told myself sternly not to get my hopes up. The television company must get hundreds of requests and they can only take on a few; and I simply didn't believe they'd be able to find Sheila. It was safer not to have any expectations so that I wasn't disappointed later. And that's all I had time to think before I fell into a sound sleep.

1

Mum Looks Like a Chinaman

I was a war baby, who used to scream when woken by the wail of the air-raid sirens and the middle-of-the-night dash for cover. Dad told me that he and Mum normally huddled under the stairs until the all-clear sounded, but one night, for some reason, he decided that we should all go to the neighbourhood shelter – and it was just as well he did because that night our house took a direct hit and the stairwell was destroyed. The top of the shelter we were in collapsed and rubble showered down on us, but no one inside was hurt. If it hadn't been for Dad's last-minute decision my story, which began with my birth in March 1943, would have been a brief one.

We'd been living in Hayes, Middlesex, but after the bombing the Red Cross billeted us with a family in Uxbridge, next to the railway line. We had the back scullery and front bedroom, and my earliest memory is of standing up in a makeshift cot, looking out the window at the lights of the trains trundling past. It must have been tough for my parents; they'd salvaged any possessions they could from the wreck of our house, but like many other families at the time they'd lost most of their furniture, kitchenware, clothes and prized personal possessions. Dad retrieved all the scrap wood he could to make new furniture, but many things simply couldn't be replaced. Meanwhile, Mum had me to take care of. She said I was a greedy baby and she struggled to get extra rations of national dried milk to feed me; I also scratched incessantly if there was wool next to my skin, but it didn't prove easy to find substitute fabrics for vests in wartime.

The war influenced us all in another way as well: I was only being brought up by my mum and dad, Dorothy and Ernest Vousden, because the woman who had given birth to me was unable to look after me. Mum said that the first time they went to see me I was in a grubby little cot wearing a dirty nightie. She and Dad couldn't have any children of their own and desperately wanted me, so they took me to live with them when I was just a few weeks old then adopted me in a court of law. This was explained right from the start, and it never bothered me in the slightest. On the contrary, I felt lucky because I had two wonderful loving parents who doted on me.

'Where is my real mum, then?' I asked Dad sometimes, and he always replied, 'In the land where the tigers grow.' That sounded reasonable to me.

We moved to Salisbury, Wiltshire, which is where I started school at Devizes Road Primary. Dad got a good job as the representative of a leading aviation company, Fairey Aviation, at RAF Boscombe Down, where top-secret experimental aircraft were tested, and Mum was a stay-at-home mother who cooked wonderful meals, baked cakes, knitted, sewed, crocheted and generally took the best of care of us. She made most of my clothes by hand and taught me how to knit and crochet myself. Once a week she washed my hair in rainwater to make it shine, and used a product called Curly Top in a futile attempt to give me curls. Her own hair was worn in what was known as a 'victory roll', sweeping off the forehead into two lavish loops on top. She was a statuesque lady who always dressed smartly, in hat and gloves, when we went out somewhere, and she made sure I looked spick and span as well.

Mum was very musical and she'd be singing as she sharpened the knives on our back doorstep, scrubbed the sheets on Monday wash day, or sewed new outfits for me on her Singer sewing machine. She taught me all the old wartime music-hall songs: 'The White Cliffs of Dover', 'Roll Out the Barrel', 'My Old Man Said Follow the Van' and 'My

Bonnie Lies Over the Ocean'. She played the piano beautifully, and at bedtime, after Dad had read me a story, Mum would play a song on the piano to lull me to sleep. My favourite was one called 'Rendezvous'. I loved to drift off with the sound of the piano floating up from downstairs.

From my earliest years, I simply loved animals. We had a Corgi called Bunty and a cat called Dinky, who stood in as my playmates since I didn't have any brothers or sisters. Horses were always my favourite, though. I used to pretend that I was riding a horse in the porch at home, and I made a beeline for any horses and donkeys I spotted when we were out. Finally, when I was eight years old, Mum let me start riding lessons at the local stables and I was overwhelmed with excitement. It was the best thing that had ever happened to me in a life that was pretty good already, and I took to the saddle like a duck to water. I wasn't spoiled, mind – I'd be swiped on the back of the legs with a hairbrush if I was misbehaving – but I was very, very loved.

Although I was christened Paulette, Dad called me his little 'Cherryanna' and the name stuck. Soon it was only teachers who called me Paulette and to everyone else I was 'Cherry'. I called him 'Pop', and I was definitely a daddy's girl, who cherished the time I spent with him. Each morning before breakfast we'd go out into the garden and walk round, inspecting the pond, deadheading the flowers and checking to see what had ripened in the vegetable patch. He'd pull up some carrots, wipe one on his hankie and hand it to me, saying, 'Eat that, Cherryanna!' In autumn he'd stretch up and pluck me a rosy apple from the tree, polishing it on his sleeve till it shone. When we went back indoors for breakfast, he'd sit on the stairs and carefully clean the mud from my shoes for me. Then on Sunday mornings, when he wasn't in a rush to get to work, I'd climb into their bed and Pop would bring up tea and chocolate biscuits and play 'camels', with me sitting on his knees and riding up and down.

He was a talented carpenter, and one of my most prized possessions was an elaborate doll's house he made me, a bungalow with a garden around it, and when you took the roof off you could see all the furniture inside. It was so detailed that there was even a little sundial in the garden, just as we had in our own garden.

I'm a visual person and all these memories are vivid pictures I carry around in my head, pictures that bring a sense of warmth and happiness and belonging. I also have a clear picture from the age of eight of a time when Mum and I were out sitting by the pond in the garden. I noticed her skin was all yellow and I said, 'Mum, you look like a Chinaman.'* Later I overheard her repeating my comment

---

* This term, which sounds racist nowadays, was in common use at the time.

to Pop and both of them laughing, but I couldn't under-stand why it was funny. No one ever mentioned the words 'liver cancer' to me, not till I was much older, and I wouldn't have known what they meant anyway.

A few weeks later, Mum had to go into hospital and I was taken to stay with some family friends, the Davidsons. I was quite happy there because I liked their son Donald, who was the same age as me; we did ballet at school together, co-starring in a production of *Sleeping Beauty*. I was going through a stage of feeling that I would rather be a boy than a girl, and Donald and I were great pals. As an only child, it was just nice to have another child in the house, someone I could play with. Mr Davidson had a film projector and we all sat and watched films in the evenings, which was great fun. I was so grateful to them for letting me stay that I tried to cook them breakfast one morning on their gas stove. In retrospect it must have been rather alarming for the family – but at least I didn't set the kitchen on fire.

I was happy enough, but in the back of my head there was a niggling worry: if Mum was ill enough to have to spend so much time in hospital, how would she ever get well again? I didn't ask anyone. I just tucked that worry inside me and carried on.

Children weren't allowed on hospital wards in those days so I couldn't visit, but once Pop drove me to the outside of the hospital and Mum came to a window near the top of the building and waved hard. She was just a tiny silhouette but it was reassuring to see her; she could still stand up and she could still wave. Hopefully that meant she wasn't too sick after all.

And then, just after my ninth birthday, Mum was allowed home from hospital and I was taken over to our house to see her. She was lying on her side of the bed in her pink flannelette nightdress, so I clambered up onto Pop's side to chat to her. There were tubes coming out of her stomach and she seemed all puffy and bloated, with pale, waxy skin. There were two bedside tables Pop had made from wood he had recovered from the bombed-out house in Hayes, and they were covered with medical paraphernalia: kidney dishes, syringes, pills and the like.

'Are you better now, Mum?' I asked, although I could tell by looking at her that she wasn't.

'No, darling,' she said quietly, her voice all hoarse and breathy. She seemed very weak, as if talking was a big struggle.

'Can I come back and stay at home with you?'

'Not yet. You're having fun at the Davidsons', aren't you?' Pop was trying to sound cheerful without much success.

I looked at the Greek key pattern of the oak headboard and listened to the rasp of Mum's breathing, trying to think of something good to say, something to make her feel better. Suddenly I had an idea. I jumped off the bed and ran round to her side of the bed, planning to give her a cuddle.

'Careful!' Pop said, putting out an arm to stop me, but not before I got round and saw that there was a white ceramic bucket full of dark red fluid on the floor, into which the tubes from Mum's stomach were draining. It didn't faze me as I've never been squeamish, but I had to watch not to kick it over.

'Can I give you a hug, Mum?' I asked. I couldn't work out how I would get my arms around her with all those tubes in the way.

She glanced at Pop and he replied: 'Not today, Cherryanna. Mum's feeling a little bit sore.'

He drove me back to the Davidsons soon after and I remember feeling very subdued. Mum had looked so tired and ill, and it wasn't like her not to give me a hug: she had always been a very tactile mum, someone who would let me climb onto her knee and snuggle up, breathing in her scent of 4711 Cologne and home baking. Now the smell around her was sharp and antiseptic and I didn't like it at all. Nothing felt right. Even Pop seemed distracted and not his usual friendly self.

At the Davidsons, I shared a bed with Rosalind, the daughter, who was a bit younger than me. It was a big old bed with an eiderdown on top. A few days after seeing Mum at home, I woke suddenly in the middle of the night and I swear I saw Mum standing at the foot of the bed. I wasn't afraid; I just looked at her, wondering what she was doing there.

'Don't worry,' she said. 'I'm an angel now but I'll still watch out for you. I will always be with you.'

I'm not sure if the voice was out loud or in my head – Rosalind didn't wake up – but I remember it very clearly, even today. Back then, in my nine-year-old's head, I knew it meant that Mum was dead and had gone to Heaven. I wasn't afraid of death because I went to Sunday school like all little children did in those days, and I believed in God and Jesus and angels in glowing white dresses with wings.

Mum's angel didn't have wings or a white dress. It was just her. It all seemed so normal that I just accepted it. She lingered at the foot of the bed for a while then faded away, and I lay awake, wondering when I would see her again and what would become of me now.

2

The New Woman
in Our Lives

Next morning, Rosalind's mum came into the bedroom and said, 'You don't need to put on your school uniform today, Cherry. Your dad's coming to take you out for the day so wear your best clothes.'

Over breakfast, Rosalind and Donald kept staring at me in a funny way and there was none of their usual joshing. I think maybe their mum or their dad had had a word before I came downstairs, telling them to be quiet. I wondered if they knew about Mum being an angel but didn't like to ask.

'Would you like some jam, Cherry?' Mr Davidson asked.

I shook my head. I didn't feel like eating anything because my tummy was aching, but I nibbled at the edge of my toast, just the tiniest of little nibbles.

Rosalind and Donald left for school and Mrs Davidson brushed my hair for me really gently, making it all shiny and neat. When Pop arrived I put on my cherry-red Sunday-best coat instead of my school coat and followed him out to the car, his old Ford Prefect with the leather seats that I loved the smell of. We drove in silence to Gulliver's, the florist opposite the hospital, and Pop pulled up outside, then hesitated, as if trying to work out what to say.

'I've got something very sad to tell you, Cherry,' he said at last, taking my hands in his, and I noticed that his eyes were red-rimmed. 'Your mummy was too sick to get better and last night I'm afraid she died.'

'Yes, I know,' I said. 'She came to see me and told me she's an angel.' I didn't feel sad at that stage because I knew she was all right – I'd seen her with my own eyes.

He looked puzzled. 'When was that?'

'Last night in bed.'

He cleared his throat. 'Anyway, we need to choose some flowers for her to hold in her coffin and I thought you might like to help me choose the prettiest ones. Will you do that?'

I nodded. We got out of the car and went into the florist, exploring the rows of big flowers and little flowers, brightly coloured and pale flowers, and in the end we decided on lily-of-the-valley because they had such a nice smell and I knew Mum had liked them.

11

Afterwards we went straight back to the Davidsons and Pop left me there with a hug, saying that he was very busy with all the arrangements but he would see me soon. I wasn't allowed to go to the funeral – children didn't go to funerals in the early fifties. I stayed at the Davidsons until the formalities were out of the way, and all that time I didn't shed a single tear. I was quiet but just got on with my schoolwork and playing with Donald and helping Mrs Davidson in the kitchen. It was only when Pop picked me up and brought me back to our house that I realised Mum really wasn't there – she wasn't in the sitting room, or in her bedroom, or in the kitchen – and I began to cry. In my nine-year-old's mind I'd somehow thought she would be, even though I knew she was an angel now. I was all muddled up.

Pop pulled me onto his lap for a hug and said, 'You mustn't cry, Cherryanna. You've got to be a very brave girl for Daddy.'

He sounded so sad that I sniffed back my snot and wiped my tears on my sleeve, swallowing the sobs in my throat. I couldn't bear to make Pop any sadder than he already was, so I zipped the emotions inside of me and locked them away, determined not to cry any more. The words 'you mustn't cry' stuck in my head, and I thought of them if I ever felt like I was going to break down, repeating them over and over to myself. 'You mustn't cry, you mustn't cry.' Pop needed me to be strong, and that's what I would be. I wanted to look after him and help him to cope. We would stick together, he and I, the two of us together, and we'd manage just fine.

Pop had other ideas, though. He couldn't manage to do his job at the aerodrome and look after a nine-year-old girl at the same time, so first of all he sent me off to stay with my auntie Florrie and uncle Sid, who lived near Margate. I don't know how long I was there but it was long enough for Auntie Florrie and me to make a knitted rabbit and stuff it full of stockings. One night I couldn't help starting to cry in bed, no matter how hard I tried not to. When Florrie came in I didn't want her to see I was upset so I squashed that rabbit hard against my face and told her to 'go away'. After that I went to stay with some friends of Pop's in Ramsgate. There was a woman living with them who had been mentally disabled since falling out of a window as a child, and she spent her days winding and unwinding cotton reels, so I used to help her.

Finally, after I don't know how long, Pop picked me up and drove me back to the house on Heath Road in Salisbury where we had lived with Mum, and it felt terribly empty without her. We took flowers to her grave and arranged them in a little crackle-glaze vase. When I looked at the mound of earth, I never believed she was in there because I knew she was an angel in Heaven. All the same, I was very upset when frost cracked the vase one week in winter and all the water spilled out and the flowers died. It seemed important to keep it looking nice for Mum.

Pop hired a succession of housekeepers to look after us, but for some reason none of them worked out. There was a couple who came to live in for a while, and I think they did their best but they couldn't compare with my mum. Nothing they did was right. For example, I liked to crunch on the raw stump in the middle of a cabbage – Mum had always given me that bit when she was making our tea. I told the housekeeper I liked it but she misunderstood and cooked the middle bit for me, boiling it till it was soft and mushy. I didn't tell her what she had done wrong but I couldn't bring myself to eat it like that. It was disgusting.

Then, on Coronation Day, 2 June 1953, there was a party in our street and everyone was getting dressed up. I had a blue-and-white-check gingham dress with a full circle skirt and red ric-rac braid round the hem that Mum had made for me before she died. I really felt the bee's knees in that dress and decided that the patriotic colours were perfect for the party. I went to school that morning then when I got back I looked for the dress and found it had been washed but not ironed, so it was all crumpled. Our housekeeper wasn't there; I was on my own in the house. I couldn't face going to the party with it looking like that, so I pulled out the ironing board and climbed on a chair to plug the iron into the light socket, the way I'd seen Mum do it. When it had heated up enough, I began to iron my favourite dress, but the creases wouldn't come out. I didn't know that some fabrics have to be dampened before ironing. I tried for ages to make it smooth and neat but it wouldn't work and I missed Mum more than ever. She would *never* have let me go out in a creased dress. With her looking after me, I was always impeccably turned out, but now there was no one to help. I went to the street party in my crumpled dress, but for me the day had a shadow cast over it and it was hard to join in the fun.

Housekeepers came and went and somehow Pop and I muddled through, but I knew he was sad. He used to get depressed when Mum was still alive, and I know they once went to the doctor to talk about it. He'd been through a lot, with our house being bombed and his having a very responsible job, but I once overheard Mum saying that he was a glass half-empty person. 'All your family are like that,' she told him. 'You believe that if the worst *can* happen, then it *will* happen.' I sort of knew what she meant, even back at that age. Now I could sense that his spirits were low again simply because he was very quiet. I was quiet too; it was a silent house.

And then one day Pop brought home a tall, scary-looking woman with carefully curled dark hair and a very posh accent, whom he introduced as Billie.

'Billie's been living in India,' Pop told me. 'And now she's back here, she's driving ambulances.'

I gazed at her.

'Do you know anything about India?' she asked.

'Isn't that where they have tigers?' I blushed. That's all I could think of.

'What's your dog's name?' she asked, and I told her it was Bunty. 'I have a bitch called Floogie,' she said. 'She was a stray and we found her one day when we were out in the ambulance, so I snuck her back to base and kept her.'

'Why did you call her Floogie?'

She smiled. 'Don't you know the song "Flat-footed Floogie with the Floy-floy"?' She turned to Pop. 'It was originally "Flat-footed Floozie", but they had to change it so the radios would play it.' They both chuckled.

I didn't know what a floozie was, never mind a floogie or a floy-floy, and I felt a bit left out. She and Pop seemed very friendly with one another and I didn't like it one bit. She was smiling at me and trying to appear kind, but there was something about her I didn't trust right from the start. I think it was because her smile didn't reach her eyes. Maybe I knew she was only pretending to be nice and didn't really feel it.

Over tea I learned that Billie had been married to an officer in the Indian Army but they'd got divorced. And then Pop dropped the bombshell. 'Billie and I have some very exciting news for you,' he said. 'We are planning to get married so that she will be like a new mummy for you. Isn't that nice? What's more, you can be the bridesmaid at our wedding.'

I grimaced. Billie was nothing like my mum and I made up my mind then and there that I would certainly never call her Mum. I didn't mind being a bridesmaid because I'd never been one before, but I worried about what their being married might entail.

'Does that mean you'll come to live in our house?' I asked, and I suppose my tone of voice didn't sound very enthusiastic.

'Don't be rude,' Pop said. 'Of course she will. We'll all be one happy family.'

It seemed to be no time at all after they broke the news that we were all trooping off to Salisbury Registry Office, me in a short flouncy dress that stuck out at the sides, and it became official: Pop and Billie were married. They took me with them for their honeymoon in Belgium, where we stayed with friends of theirs, and I felt utterly lost and alone in the world. Pop had been my only ally and now he was lavishing all his attention on this posh woman I hardly knew. We were in a strange country, with strange people speaking a different language, and I felt completely cut off. *If only I had a brother or sister*, I thought. *At least we'd be in this together. We could have ganged up and played tricks on her, and kept each other company.*

Billie was nice to me on the honeymoon, trying to play-act at being my new mum, but on the way home we stopped at a hotel in Dover, where she decided to cut my shoulder-length hair. 'It's far too much trouble to look after,' she said by way of explanation. She had been a hairdresser herself before she got married the first time, and she wielded the scissors, giving me a short crop that made me look like a boy. I gazed at my reflection in the mirror, remembering all the care Mum had lavished on my hair, and I knew things were only going to get worse from here on in.

3

My Closest Friend, Grizelda the Goat

At first Billie's influence was just felt in terms of strictness about the way she ran the household. She was constantly chiding me to speak 'properly' and adopt a posh accent like hers instead of the Wiltshire one of my schoolmates; I wasn't allowed to mix with anyone she didn't consider to be of 'our class'; and at seven shillings a week she decided that my riding lessons were far too expensive and had to be stopped. I was distraught about this and begged her to reconsider, but she said things like 'needs must' and 'don't be a spoiled little girl', which meant there was no room for discussion.

Before long I was constantly on edge, waiting to be told what I had done wrong, and Pop never intervened to support me; he was a gentle, go-with-the-flow person who was soon totally under Billie's thumb. We hardly had any time alone together anymore because he was out at work during the day, and when he came home Billie was there. I remember once he took me to the airfield at Boscombe Down, and I was allowed to climb into the cockpit of Fairey Delta 2, a new plane that had just broken the world speed record. It had a long pointy nose and was very narrow. Inside, I sat in the pilot's seat, holding onto the steering column and looking at the figures on all the dials; one of these dials had recorded the speed of 1,132 miles per hour that it had achieved to break the record. I tried to imagine what it must have felt like to be in the pilot's seat then as the world whizzed past. That was a pretty special treat.

After I showed an interest in Fairey Delta 2, Dad told me about the rickety little planes he used to work on in the First World War. 'Like string bags made out of balsa wood and cloth treated with dope,' he said, which made them terrible fire hazards. He'd been a Flight Sergeant with 56 Squadron and had fitted out planes in France, then when the war ended he'd gone on a goodwill flight to South Africa with dozens of stops along the way – he showed me them on the map. After that he went out to work on planes in India for a couple of years. I was in awe of this. It seemed terribly glamorous to be an aeroplane fitter back in the days when aviation was in its infancy.

Sometimes Pop would sneak into my bedroom and wake me in the middle of the night if there was a nightingale singing outside, or if there was a particularly dramatic thunderstorm he thought I'd like to watch. We were both fans of thunder and lightning. But otherwise Billie was always around and always criticising both of us.

With Pop, her main complaint was that he didn't earn enough money to keep her in the style to which she had become accustomed in India. Our Salisbury home was a perfectly nice semi-detached house with a beautiful garden, but Billie wanted something grander where she could be a lady of the manor. She persuaded Pop to buy Glebe House in West Lavington, a gorgeous old property which was actually three cottages knocked into one. It stood in three-quarters of an acre of garden with a trout stream running through it. I think this was a stretch for them to afford because Billie insisted that I paid for my own bedroom with the £200 Mum had left me in her will, which was in a building society account in my name.

I liked the West Lavington house, especially after Billie got a goat, which we kept in a shed in the garden. I became very close to that goat, who was named Grizelda. I never talked about my emotions to any human beings – I saw it as a sign of weakness now, something that could be used against me – but I always found solace in animals, and Grizelda was an exceptionally good listener. Every day, when I got home from school, I'd take out the vegetable peelings for her and sit telling her about my day; I'd talk about any girls who'd been mean to me, or teachers who were cross, or complain about the amount of homework we had. Grizelda would munch on her carrot tops, regarding me with a wise expression, then bend her head for me to scratch it. She genuinely was my best friend and confidante through those early teenage years.

I did try to make other friends. Someone told me about a youth club in West Lavington, something to do with the Methodist church, where you could play games and hang out with other kids the same age. Surely Billie would let me join that? It was local so I could walk there myself.

'We will both go along together,' she ruled when I told her about it. 'I will judge whether or not it is suitable.'

I imagined her charging in, wearing her fur coat and full make-up, turning up her nose at the club, announcing that they were the 'wrong sort of people', while I tried to hide behind her in my embarrassment. Cringing, I said, 'No, I've changed my mind. I don't think I'll bother after all.'

I hadn't forgotten my love of horses, and I found that if I turned up at the local stables every weekend to muck out, they let me have a ride every now and then. There was a field of horses very near our house and sometimes I would sneak out with a halter I'd made out of string and ride around on one of them. I was never happier than when I was out on horseback with the wind in my hair. When you're out there on a horse, you have to be able to deal with whatever happens, and I was learning a lot about being self-sufficient. I was getting good at it.

After leaving Devizes Road Primary I attended Devizes Grammar School, a co-ed some distance away from home. Every morning I had to catch a bus then walk a mile and a half, which inevitably got me there late, doing the same on the way home. It was difficult to make friends since I lived so far from school and wasn't allowed to invite anyone home, or to take part in after-school activities. Billie had other plans for me: unpaid housework. I did the washing, the ironing, the cleaning, fed the dogs, prepared the vegetables for dinner every evening and washed up afterwards. I guess she'd had servants to do all these things in India, and in West Lavington I became the substitute *punkah-wallah*.

Soon I began to rebel, and we clashed bitterly. I was distraught when I came home from school one day to find that Billie had retrieved my old doll's house from the attic, driven a stake through it and turned it into a bird table in the garden.

'What are you so upset about?' she asked. 'You didn't play with it anymore.'

'I wanted to keep it. It was my special thing that Pop made me. How could you destroy it?'

'At least it's doing some good now instead of just taking up space.' She failed to understand its emotional significance, and when I told Pop that evening he just shrugged and sighed and opened his paper. He'd do anything to avoid a fight.

Billie didn't ever beat me but she locked me in my bedroom as punishment for misdemeanours, not realising that I could slither through the bars at the window and jump down onto the roof of the goat shed below. I suppose in retrospect I was a bit of a rebel.

One flashpoint was clothes: whereas my mum had bought me a new coat and new shoes every year because I was a 'growing girl', Billie complained about the cost of things. She would never buy me the correct school uniform, instead sending me to school in a hotch-potch of garments, for which the teachers told me off. My out-of-school clothes were all frumpy hand-me-downs from Billie's sister, which Billie insisted that I 'make do with and mend'. When I complained, she retorted, 'What do you want nice clothes for? You've got a face like a spade.'

One of our worst fights came after I got home from school one day to find that Grizelda was gone.

'Where is she?' I screamed. 'What have you done with Grizelda?'

'She got on my nerves, eating everything in the garden,' Billie said, 'so I gave her away to a farmer.'

'Which farmer? Where is she?' I wouldn't stop my persistent questioning until Billie gave in and told me where Grizelda had been rehomed, then I charged out of the house and walked all the way there. When Grizelda saw me she got so excited she tried to leap over the fence. I hugged her and cried, but had no choice but to leave her there when it was time to go home again. I missed her terribly after that.

When I asked, in typical teenage fashion, 'What about me? Don't my feelings come into it?' Billie replied, crushingly: 'You? You're less than a grain of sand in the universe.'

Only once did Pop stand up for me in a fight with Billie. We were in the car and I was begging her to buy me some summer stockings rather than the awful 60-denier nylon pair I was supposed to make last for an entire school year. 'Who do you think you are? Lady Muck?' Billie rebuked. 'We're not made of money, you know.' Suddenly, Pop screeched the car to a halt and yelled, 'You will not treat her like that. Get out of the car!' There was a blazing row, but for once he stood his ground and made Billie walk the three miles home.

When I was around fourteen, Pop was made redundant from his job as representative of Fairey Aviation when they closed down that branch of the aircraft testing site at Boscombe Down. He could have retired at that stage, but Billie persuaded him that they wouldn't have enough money to live on from his pension. She had very expensive tastes, particularly in home décor, constantly changing our carpets, curtains and upholstery for the latest shades and styles. She insisted that Pop went back to work in the aerodrome storeroom, which was a huge climbdown for someone who had been in charge, and I could tell he hated it. We downsized to a house in Amesbury, Wiltshire, and I moved to the South Wilts Grammar School for Girls for my third year onwards.

The overwhelming feeling in my teens was loneliness and isolation. My contemporaries in the late fifties and early sixties were listening to pop music, wearing the latest fashions and going to dances where live bands played, but I had no social life except accompanying Pop and Billie to evenings spent playing cards with their friends. Every day after school my classmates hung out in the Red Cockerel coffee shop, chatting to boys and having a laugh. I yearned to join them but my pocket money was all taken up paying for school lunches, and besides, I'd have been in big trouble if I missed the bus home. I sat in the window seat of the bus watching them all clustered round a table in the Red Cockerel and felt like an alien species. It was such a lonely feeling.

In the early years of their marriage they had talked, tantalisingly, about adopting a child because Billie couldn't have any of her own, and she said she'd always wanted to have a son. They made enquiries but Billie found the adoption agency's assessment procedures rude and intrusive.

'These flipping people, they want to come and inspect our house and ask all sorts of personal questions about us, and they haven't even let me see what kind of child they might have available. I'm not putting up with this!' she exclaimed.

My chance of gaining an ally, someone I could be close to, were dashed. After that my only hope was escape, to start a life of my own somewhere I could make my own choices and determine my own fate.

4

A Hasty Marriage

I passed two A Levels in sixth form and hoped to study agriculture at college, to pursue my love of animals. Billie objected to this plan, though – 'It's no career for a young lady' – and instead I was signed up to study horticulture at Nottingham, which she deemed more fitting. That summer Dad and Billie moved to Deal in Kent (he had finally retired completely from the aerodrome), and it was while we were living there that Billie decided to become a Jehovah's Witness.

She had always had her religious fads: there was a spiritualism phase, then a faith-healing phase to help ease the arthritis she suffered from, but the Jehovah's Witness phase was the worst of all. She was obsessive about reading *The Watchtower* and going out to try to convert our neighbours, which was a total embarrassment. She banged on about modesty and virtue, railing against drunkenness and promiscuity, gambling and tobacco, and it was like listening to a record with the needle stuck in a groove. I don't know how Pop put up with it; all I could do was leave home.

It was a requirement of my horticulture course that I completed a year's practical work, so I managed to get a job at Mount Nurseries in Canterbury where my life became fun for the first time since Mum died. I moved into digs, and soon I'd made loads of friends among the other staff at the nursery. We all went to the pub together in the evenings after work. There were a few boyfriends, nothing serious, and fun social events almost every night of the week. I felt as though I'd been let out of jail! I was skint most of the time because there was hardly anything left of my wages after the fifteen shillings a week I paid for board and lodgings, but I was having the time of my life.

At first I got the bus home every weekend to visit Billie and Pop, but the final straw in my relationship with my stepmother came over a cucumber sandwich, of all things. I'd travelled home and was hungry when I arrived, so I went into the kitchen to make said sandwich.

'What do you think you are doing? You eat far too much!' Billie snapped.

I looked at her, buttery knife poised in my hand in mid-air, and simply thought, 'I don't want this anymore.' I'd been shoved down by her all through my teens, and now that I was starting to pull myself up I refused to be squashed any more.

I put down the knife, left the sandwich behind on the countertop, walked out the door and never went back to that house again. From then on, Pop had to travel to Canterbury to see me – and, bless him, he did come regularly, although he admitted that it made things 'a bit tricky' with Billie. (She later accused him of having an affair with my landlady simply because he put up a kitchen cupboard for her!)

Now that I was my own boss I decided not to study horticulture after all because going to university would have meant I'd still be partly financially dependent on Pop and Billie, and I didn't want any further involvement with that woman. Instead, I looked for jobs in the newspaper and finally decided to apply to study radiography at Canterbury Hospital, where you could train in-house. I was lucky to be accepted by the lugubrious consultant radiologist Dr Johnson, even though I didn't have A Level Maths, and I enjoyed hospital life straight away.

It was around this time that I was introduced by a mutual friend to a man named Eric. He was quite a bit older than me, had been a professional footballer and was now practising as a chiropodist in a surgery near my digs. I thought nothing of it when my friend introduced us, but soon I noticed that Eric always seemed to be standing outside when I walked past and would call me over for a chat. One day he invited me to accompany him to a cricket match in which he was playing, so I went along and somehow we just fell into being boyfriend and girlfriend.

There was no great romance. I felt a sense of security with him because he knew more than me about the way the world worked, he was qualified and had a good career, and he seemed to have his whole life planned out. I was still only nineteen years old and, although I didn't regret the decision to stop having any contact with Billie, I felt very alone in the world, with no one to fall back on should things go wrong. That's where Eric came in. I thought he would look after me, so two years later when he asked me if I wanted to get engaged, I just said yes. He bought me a diamond ring from an antique shop – quite a decent diamond, it was – which cost £21 (a substantial amount in those days).

In the mid-sixties, late teens to early twenties was the normal age for girls to get married – leave it too late and people described you as being 'on the shelf' – and I thought I'd better not miss my chance. The landlady at my digs tried to talk me out of it. 'Are you sure you're doing the right thing?' she asked. 'He's quite a lot older than you.' But my mind was made up simply because, to me, marriage to Eric would mean security. It's what girls my age did.

Pop came alone to the registry office ceremony in September 1964. I'd bought myself a blue dress, jacket, hat and a pair of shoes in a charity shop, all for three pounds, and my landlady took some photographs in which I look about fifty years old! Standing in front of the registrar, I got my first shock of married life when Eric was asked for his date of birth. As he gave it, I did the arithmetic in my head and realised that he was five years older than I'd thought: thirty-three rather than twenty-eight, making him twelve years my senior. I didn't say anything, though. I looked at him open-mouthed but didn't like to make a fuss.

We went for lunch in the Falstaff Hotel in Canterbury – Pop, his sister Blanche, Eric and me. Eric's family lived in Doncaster and couldn't travel down for the wedding. Immediately after lunch, Eric and I walked back up the road to strip wallpaper in a house we'd just bought and were doing up. There was no honeymoon; it was straight down to the business of being 'a married couple'.

Ours was a typical 1950s marriage, a decade too late; although women across the nation were starting to burn their bras, there was certainly none of your Women's Lib in our household! I did all the shopping, cooking and cleaning while carrying on with my radiography studies, and Eric worked in his chiropody practice during the day then played golf and cricket with his mates in the evening and at weekends.

My weak spot was that I desperately wanted a family, to find somewhere I belonged. When I visited friends' families I used to analyse the dynamics, trying to figure out how they worked, because family life was something I hadn't experienced since Mum died. I yearned for lots of children to make a big happy gang in which I was a core member, so I mucked in and cooked and cleaned and did my absolute best to make my marriage a success.

All the same, I remember one moment, a few weeks after the wedding, when I was in a little room at the hospital where I was training. There was a brown rug on the floor, and I stared at it and thought, 'What have I done?' Although I'd been dating Eric for two years, agreeing to marry him had been impulsive; it had seemed like something I *should* do rather than something I *wanted* to do, and now the reality of the decades stretching in front of me seemed daunting. There was nothing to be done about it, though, so I just snapped myself out of that introspective mood and got on with things.

Soon after the wedding, Pop came to visit, bringing with him a folder of papers. He handed them over, saying, 'I thought it's about time you should have these.'

I opened the folder and flicked through. There was a lengthy correspondence with Reginald Johnson & Co Solicitors in Hayes, Middlesex, regarding 'The Adoption of Paulette' – and I realised with a start that it was all about me. For some reason my heart started to pound.

It seemed that although I had been born in March 1943 and had gone to live with Mum and Pop (Dorothy and Ernest Vousden) six weeks later, I had not been officially adopted by them until March 1944 because my birth father had been in the army and they hadn't been able to track him down to get his signature on the paperwork. There was a copy of a sad little letter on blue writing paper from my mum to my birth father, sent care of his unit: 'We are anxious to adopt her but cannot do so without your written consent, would you kindly do this without further delay & so enable us to get the matters settled.'

It struck me immediately how heart-rending it must have been for Mum and Pop to bring me up for a whole year – doing the nappies and the night feeds, bathing and dressing me – while, at any time, my birth parents could have come to claim me back because the adoption was not formalised. That must have been very stressful for them. How could you let yourself love a baby you might not be able to keep? Yet there was no doubt that Mum and Pop had loved me without reservation from the minute they took me home with them.

'We were pretty sure they wouldn't come back for you,' Pop agreed, 'but it was certainly a relief when it was all finalised. Your mother and I had been trying for a long time for a baby – since our marriage in 1922 – so as you can imagine we couldn't wait to have it all confirmed legally.'

'Twenty-one years!' I exclaimed. 'That must have been so hard for you.'

'It was a particular sorrow for your mother. I had my work but she just had her home to run, and I think she felt it very keenly when friends were talking about their children's achievements. Thank God she had the nine years of looking after you. It made her so happy.'

I smiled, remembering what a wonderful mother she had been. I was very lucky in that sense … not so much in others.

Next I looked at the four-page certificate that legally made me the child of Dorothy and Ernest Vousden under the 1926 Adoption of Children Act. On the third page, in black and white, there were the names of my birth mother and father: Daisy Louise Noël of Shelburne Road, High Wycombe, and Henri Le Gresley Noël of Saighton Camp, near Chester. I got goosebumps on my arms looking at them.

'Why do their names sound so foreign?' I asked.

'They were from Jersey,' Pop explained. 'Daisy was evacuated in 1940 when the Germans were about to invade the Channel Islands. Henri was in the army. I believe their marriage failed and she didn't feel capable of raising a child on her own, especially during wartime.'

'Poor Daisy,' I said, trying to imagine what it must be like to give up your baby. I pictured her in floods of tears as she handed over the bundle swathed in a pristine white blanket.

The last page of the certificate was about wills; it explained that adopted children bore all the same rights as children born naturally to a couple, except that they would not automatically inherit any estate unless there was a will naming them as heirs.

'Don't worry; you are named as my heir,' Pop said. 'Not that there's much to inherit.'

He looked tired, and I'd noticed he was getting forgetful. When I was younger I'd never minded having older parents, but now I was in my twenties, Dad was in his sixties and starting to succumb to the niggling ailments of old age.

'Thanks for bringing these, Pop,' I said. I couldn't stop looking at those names – Daisy and Henri Le Gresley Noël. What ages would they be now and what were they doing with their lives?

And then a thought struck me: perhaps they had gone on to remarry and have more children. I might have half-brothers and sisters somewhere. Wouldn't that be lovely! I daydreamed about discovering a big extended family of cousins and aunties, grandparents, nephews and nieces, who all met up for Christmases and birthdays and weddings. Then I snapped myself out of it. I still had a wonderful dad, and I'd once had the best mum in the world; lots of people couldn't say as much. I should count myself lucky and not hanker after anything more.

5

Learning to Be a Mum

It was fascinating to learn that my birth parents came from Jersey, meaning that I had a connection with the Channel Islands. I knew very little about the wartime occupation there, but I went to the library and did some reading to try to understand what the people had been through. I read that after the Fall of France in June 1940 and its occupation by German troops, the British government decided they couldn't spare the manpower to defend the islands, which were much closer to France than they were to Britain. Everyone was aware that it would give the Germans a propaganda coup to say they had conquered part of the British Isles, but there would be no particular strategic advantages for them in having a base there and the islands would simply be too tricky for the British Army to defend.

Each island had its own governing body, and in those rushed, chaotic days of mid-June 1940 they all adopted different policies towards evacuation. Alderney officials recommended that everyone be evacuated; Sark urged everyone to stay; on Guernsey they decided to evacuate all school-age children; on Jersey the advice was to stay, and most followed it, with only around a tenth of the population deciding to leave – including, I supposed, my birth mother. Boats left the islands for the UK mainland between 20 and 23 June 1940, and the Germans took possession on 1 July, so it was all a big rush. I looked at photographs of old women sobbing as they waved at departing boats, of little children perched on their fathers' shoulders looking bewildered, of decks crammed with people looking fearful, unsure of what awaited them on the mainland. It must have been a terrifying choice: wait for the Germans or leap into the unknown and start a new life.

By the time I was born, my mother, Daisy, was in England and my father was off fighting somewhere. According to the adoption certificate her address was in Shelburne Road, High Wycombe. I knew High Wycombe because my Auntie Wyn (Mum's sister) and Uncle Frank used to live there. I remembered their next-door neighbours kept chickens and goats in a big uncultivated garden, and I liked to climb over and play with them even though Aunt Wyn kept telling me not to.

'Stay out, Cherry. You'll annoy them,' she chided. But I had always loved goats and I was straight over that fence whenever she wasn't looking, even after one of the goats butted me and knocked me to the ground.

I wondered if an adoption agency had given me to my mum and dad – the adoption papers didn't name one. Alternatively, perhaps Auntie Wyn had known Daisy and told her about this couple who couldn't have children of their own and were desperate to adopt. Was that how it all happened?

For a brief moment I considered writing to the Shelburne Road address to ask if the current occupants had a forwarding address for Daisy, but then I changed my mind. I felt sure Pop would be upset if I tried to contact my birth parents. It was almost like saying that he wasn't a good enough dad. I couldn't do that to him, and I certainly didn't want to do it behind his back, so I put the adoption papers away in a drawer.

Meanwhile, Eric and I were keen to start a family of our own. In the spring of 1965 I had a miscarriage, which was very distressing, but luckily by the end of the year I was pregnant again. I gave birth to my daughter Helen in April 1966, and it was then that I realised I knew absolutely nothing about babies! I'd had no contact with them, and while most girls could ask their mothers for help and advice, I had no one to ask and simply had to muddle through. For example, I didn't know that your milk doesn't come in for three days; I had no idea what to do when Helen was obviously hungry and I had hardly anything in my breasts to feed her. (I'd decided from the start that I wanted to breastfeed, even though it wasn't the fashion at the time, because to me it felt more natural. That's what we have breasts for, isn't it?)

There was no one you could ask in those days. I'd met a few women at antenatal classes and we exchanged notes, but they were mostly young and clueless like me. I felt a complete amateur but somehow I managed to master breast-feeding, then weaning her on mashed bananas and stewed apples. There was endless hand-washing of terry towelling nappies in a sink down in the basement then struggling to get them dry because there was no heating in the house. When my son Graham came along in December 1967, I was an old hand at rearing babies and it all went more smoothly, although there were double the number of nappies to wash.

Our house in Canterbury was a Victorian building, four storeys tall. On the ground floor was the surgery and waiting room for Eric's chiropody practice. I had to share the only bathroom, on the first floor, with all the old ladies who'd come in to have their feet done, and I hated that. The kitchen was on the same level as the surgery, and our sitting/dining room was on the top floor so if we sat down to dinner and I realised I'd forgotten the salt, it was a trek down four flights of stairs to retrieve it then another four flights back up again. It obviously wasn't an ideal house in which to live with two babies; when I arrived home with a pram, several bags of shopping and the two of them wailing for a feed, there was many a time I could have done with an extra pair of arms.

I had loads of memories of my own mum – how warm and cuddly she had been, the feeling of safety when I was snuggling on her lap and the peacefulness of lying in bed, tucked under the covers, while she played the piano to lull me to sleep. I wasn't very good at doing these things for my own children, though. I did all the physical, practical things – feeding, washing, clothing, nursing them when they were sick, taking them for dental check-ups and registering them for schools – but emotionally I felt shut off. I think it went back to the first time I returned to the house after Mum's death, when I was sitting on Pop's knee and he told me not to cry but to be a brave girl. In everything that had happened to me since then, I'd suppressed my emotions and simply coped, so when it came to my own children I found I was unable to be demonstrative and loving. We weren't a cuddly family, although I loved them to pieces.

Apart from anything else, I was always short of time. Eric liked his routines: breakfast on the table at eight, lunch at twelve, supper at six, so looking after the kids had to fit around that. I had finished my radiography course before getting pregnant, but there was no part-time radiography work in our area, so instead I took odd jobs to make money. In summer I'd be out fruit-picking while the kids snoozed in their prams or toddled around trying to help; in winter I made teddy bears for a market stall, stuffing them, sewing them up and sticking in those eerie glass eyes.

Eric gave me housekeeping money (when we first married it was four shillings a week) but it was a struggle to feed and clothe all of us. I economised where I could, only buying my own clothes from charity shops. Once, Eric and I were invited to a posh do at the golf club and I bought a second-hand gold brocade dress, full-length and fitted, from Oxfam; I was quite pleased with it but he complained: 'What if we get there and someone else recognises it as theirs?' Fortunately they didn't – or at least if they did, they were too polite to say.

Life was one big juggling act of housework, childcare, trying to earn money, and marriage to a man who had old-fashioned ideas about a woman's role. Mostly I was too submissive to kick up a fuss.

6

Breaking Out of Domesticity

Little by little, bit by bit, I began to lift myself out of the role of domestic skivvy and stay-at-home mum. Once the children started school, I signed myself up for a correspondence course in chiropody. Eric approved, because it would mean I could help with some of the home visits needed in his practice, travelling out on my bicycle to see clients who were unable to attend the surgery.

When I'd qualified as a chiropodist and was earning some decent sums of money on my own account, I could supplement the housekeeping. Helen was doing dance classes, which she loved, and there were always extras she needed for the regular shows. Now I could buy these and I could pay for Graham to take riding lessons at the local stables. I began to put my foot down about certain things around the house as well. In particular, I'd always wanted a washing machine but Eric didn't see the need: 'My mother managed perfectly well without a washing machine so why can't you?'

Instead of arguing I saved the money from my wages then slipped into the Co-op in town and chose a modest Indesit automatic, giving strict instructions that it was not to be delivered until the following day, which would give me enough time to prepare Eric for the arrival.

Imagine my horror when I arrived home to find some men already unloading the machine from the back of a van and trundling it noisily towards our front steps!

'No, not that way!' I cried. 'Quick – come round the back.'

They installed the washing machine in the basement and, after a spot of grumbling, Eric accepted it once it was there. This gave me the idea of having a fitted kitchen installed while he was off on a golfing holiday. He could hardly rip it out again once it was in place, I reckoned (although he did complain that it was a shocking waste of money!).

These little bits of progress gave me confidence. With each tiny step forwards, my life was becoming a bit easier. With the children both at school, I had some hours free and my day wasn't complete drudgery from morning to night. My next purchase was a huge secret, one I knew that Eric would never have consented to in a million years: I bought myself a horse.

It had been one of my childhood dreams to own a horse, and there was a field down by the river in Canterbury where I used to stop and pet the horses. I got talking to the old chap there and he told me he was look-ing to loan one of his horses, a thoroughbred named Ferica, for four pounds a week. Straight away I agreed to take it on, then a while later I bought a sorry-looking four-year-old called Copper at a horse fair in Ashford, only to find out later that it was a par-bred American quarter horse. I still don't know how I got away with rush-ing out to groom, feed and ride the horses every day; I just got on my bike and went, and Eric never asked questions. It was a huge deception but I loved my horses to pieces and they brought me a lot of happy times. I finally had to confess to Eric a couple of years later, after I arrived home splattered from head to foot in mud, and he was utterly speechless, too gobsmacked even to protest.

Later still I took driving lessons. Eric didn't drive and wasn't keen on me learning, but I persevered and, after I passed the test, managed to buy myself a beat-up old car, a pale blue Singer Chamois, which cost £120. It was a lovely car with a walnut dashboard, but sadly it got writ-ten off a few years later when an uninsured student drove into me on a country road. I liked the independence driving brought, but for local journeys I'd always use my trusty old bike.

Still I found it difficult to show affection for my children. I'd have fought to the death to protect either of them, and I worked my socks off to buy whatever material things they needed, but I was such a squashed, bruised apple of a person that I was incapable of hugging them or telling them that I loved them. I'd do the chores instead of taking them to the park, accept extra bookings at work instead of having a day out at a fun fair, and I bitterly regret that now. You'd think losing my mum would have made me extra loving towards my own children, but with me it worked in quite the opposite way, making me cautious and reserved. It was a loss for them, and a loss for me too because I missed the chance to enjoy being a mum.

In 1975, I read a story in the newspapers that made me prick up my ears. Under a new law, adopted people had the right to apply for their birth certificates and seek information about the agency involved in their adoption, with a view to tracking down their birth parents. I still didn't plan to track down Daisy and Henri Noël because I didn't want to hurt Pop's feelings, but I thought I should apply for a copy of my birth certificate. Apart from anything else, I thought I'd need it if I ever wanted to get a passport. You had to have counselling first, so I made an appointment and went along on the day to find a young, wet-behind-the-ears lad sitting behind a big desk, looking rather embarrassed by the role in which he found himself.

'Do you think you are prepared for this?' he asked, peering at a form in front of him.

'Yes,' I replied. My heart was pounding, but I didn't want to tell this lad I was nervous and have to listen to him spouting counselling clichés he'd memorised from a textbook.

'Are you sure?'

'Yeah.'

He opened a file, pulled out the certificate and passed it over, saying, 'Here you are, then.' So much for counselling!

I don't know why I'd been nervous. The long, horizontal sheet didn't give me much information that I hadn't already gleaned from my adoption certificate, but I did learn that my birth mother's maiden name was Daisy Louise Banks and that she came from Bellozanne Valley in Jersey, that my father's occupation was itinerant farm worker and that he'd grown up in Ville à l'Evêque, Jersey. I now had addresses where they had lived at some stage, and once again I vaguely considered sending out tentative letters to make contact. I did try writing to the army authorities, trying to find out about my birth father's military career, but my letters got passed from one department to the next without bringing any solid information.

I wanted to know about Daisy and Henri, but I decided it wasn't fair on Pop to try to get in contact with them directly.

Pop and Billie had just moved up to Scarborough, her home town, and he was becoming increasingly forgetful. We wrote to each other but often his letters contained non sequiturs or things that simply didn't make sense. When I phoned, it was always Billie who answered, and if she passed the phone to him he frequently seemed confused. Even if I'd felt I could ask him questions about my birth parents, he probably wouldn't have been able to answer them now. I'd missed my chance to ask whether he ever met Daisy Banks Noël, and whether she had been introduced to them by Auntie Wyn and Uncle Frank.

One day, I remembered that Pop had once given me a Jersey half-sovereign and told me he had dug it up in the garden. It was gold and glittery, like buried pirate treasure, and I'd kept it in his collar stud box. Suddenly, I began to wonder if that had been a parting gift from either Daisy or Henri as they said goodbye to their baby daughter. (Actually, I wasn't sure whether Henri had ever set eyes on me or if he was away at the front when I was born. That seems more likely, because had he been around he could have signed those adoption papers straight away and saved Mum and Pop a year of heartache and worry.)

I tried asking Pop about the half-sovereign but he just looked blank, his memory being stolen bit by bit by the ravages of what was later diagnosed as dementia.

7

Searching for My Birth Father

One morning in the early 1980s, I was browsing through the local paper at the kitchen table when my eye was caught by an article about how to trace your family. They had interviewed an amateur genealogist called John Stroud about methods he used to find missing relatives and draw up family trees. He used local history libraries, newspaper archives, church records and the official registers of births, marriages and deaths, and had achieved some notable successes in reuniting family members who hadn't seen each other for years.

I tore the page out of the paper and slipped it in my pocket because I was rushing out to the horses and didn't want to risk Eric throwing the paper away before I got back. Later on, I reread the article. Mr Stroud sounded very approachable and I decided to write to him, care of the paper, to see if he could find out anything about my birth family. Still, I just wanted information. In particular, I wondered if Daisy and Henri Noël had remarried and I might have half-brothers or sisters somewhere.

A week later I got a reply from Mr Stroud saying he would be happy to help me trace my birth parents. He asked for copies of my adoption documents and my birth certificate. I'd asked what fee he would charge for helping me, but he replied that he wouldn't charge me anything. Genealogy was a hobby for him. I made the copies and sent them to him in the very next post, feeling both excited and nervous at the same time. I hadn't thought through what I would do if he did find them, but I desperately hoped we would be able to form some kind of relationship. Pop's health was declining and there was no need for him to find out what I was doing, so it couldn't hurt him.

John Stroud did his best, He wrote that his daughter had personally gone in to the Register Office in London to do a search for them but hadn't been able to find anything. Since we didn't know their dates of birth, it was like looking for a needle in a haystack. None of his other searches had turned up any leads and he wrote: 'The trouble is that all the information you've given me about Daisy and Henri is almost forty years out of date. After that length of time it's not surprising if you can't find any neighbours who remember them, and I wouldn't expect anyone to have forwarding addresses for them. We'll keep trying though, Cherry.'

He was a lovely man who always broke bad news to me in the most sensitive ways, remaining cheerful and positive throughout. However, after several weeks of dead ends, we agreed there was nowhere else to go at the UK end.

Meanwhile, I'd had another idea. Both Daisy and Henri had been born in Jersey, as far as I knew, so perhaps I would have more luck if I wrote to the Register Office in St Helier. I sent a request for their birth certificates, along with a cheque, and it was such a long time before I heard anything more that I had all but given up hope by the time a long, official-looking envelope plopped through the letterbox. I opened it and found a birth certificate inside. With great excitement I realised it was for my father, Henri Le Gresley Noël. According to this piece of paper, he was the son of Philippe Noël, a labourer, and Louisa Mary Ann Le Breton in the parish of Trinity in Jersey. His birthday was 4 January 1913. It was now 1982, which meant he was sixty-nine years old and there was a good chance he was still alive. I crossed my fingers that he would be.

Now that I had my biological father's date of birth, I was able to apply to the British Register Office again to see if they had any marriage certificates in his name. At least he had an unusual name, and the chances of getting the wrong person were slight. He and my mother had separated by the time I was born in 1943, when he was thirty years old. Surely he would have remarried in the last thirty-nine years? And surely there was a good chance he had had more children?

It seemed to take ages before another certificate arrived, telling me that he had married a woman called Dora in 1964 and that they had lived in Cardiff. There was an address in St Mellons, a district in the northeast of the city.

Now for the moment of truth. I had a chance to get in touch with my birth father, but what on earth would I say? Who was he, anyway? Why had he split up with my birth mother? Why hadn't he wanted me? There were so many questions I needed answers to and the only thing for it was to write.

I kept my letter very short and factual, just asking if he had been married to Daisy Banks from Jersey and saying that, if so, I thought I might be his daughter. I told him I had been adopted in April 1943 by a lovely couple, Dorothy and Ernest Vousden and that I was now married with two children of my own, but that I was curious to find out about his side of the family and would be very grateful if he was willing to enter into a correspondence with me. I addressed the envelope, licked the stamp and went out to the postbox. I hesitated for a minute, holding the envelope in the slot but not letting it go. And then I relaxed my fingers and heard the plop as it hit the other mail piled at the bottom. Now for the waiting.

In fact, it didn't take very long before I heard back. Somehow I knew from the unfamiliar handwriting on the envelope that it was a reply to my letter, and I ripped it open to find a small sheet of beige paper covered on both sides in curly writing in blue Biro.

'*Dear Paulette,*' it read. '*Your letter was forwarded on to me from St Mellons. I'm sorry to say your dad died eight years ago. It was the anniversary of his death yesterday, 6 Aug.*'

I gasped and dropped the page, a huge lump in my throat. What a shame I hadn't tried to contact him earlier, back when Pop first brought me the adoption papers. It felt like a horribly cruel trick of fate to let me build up my hopes about Henri Le Gresley Noël. Of course, he could never have been a substitute for Pop, the lovely father I'd grown up with, but I'd hoped we would have felt a bond of sorts and that he could have filled in some missing links for me about my past. I'd been curious to meet him and see what he looked like, hear what he spoke like – but sadly it wasn't to be.

When I had recovered my composure, I noticed that there were some photographs in the envelope from Dora

Noël and I pulled them out. I blinked hard as I looked at them. They were obviously holiday snaps showing a man with a startling, uncanny resemblance to my husband Eric. They had the same high forehead and widow's peak, the eyes were slightly close together and there was a kind of Germanic look about them. I was shocked to the core. How could I have chosen to marry someone the spitting image of my father when I had never even met or seen a picture of him? Is it possible that he was there when I was born or had visited in the few weeks before Mum and Pop adopted me, and I'd somehow retained a visual memory of him since babyhood then sought out a partner who looked the same way? Was there some kind of genetic predisposition in my DNA to choose men with that kind of look? Or was it just a bizarre coincidence? It certainly made me feel very strange.

One of the photos showed Dad with Dora, and I saw she was a very attractive dark-haired woman with looks that seemed almost Mediterranean. I went back to read the rest of her letter. She told me that just after the war, my father had married her cousin Lil, and that they'd had a daughter called Susan (known to all as Sue). So that meant I had a half-sister! Lil had died when Sue was eleven, so she and I had something in common: both of us had lost our mothers at an early age. During her teenage years she had been looked after by her dad and her gran. Henri Noël had then got remarried, to Dora, at the end of 1964 and they had nine happy years together before he died of cancer in 1974. It sounded as though Dora was close to Sue and her family; she mentioned that she had just been down to visit them in North Devon.

Dora wrote about my father: 'He was a good, kind man, very energetic and fond of gardening.' She said she was still in touch with his younger sister Ada – my aunt – who lived in Jersey, and offered to give me her address. She also said she would be happy to put me in touch with Sue and to answer any further questions I might like to ask, finishing by saying, 'I'm sorry you never knew your dad.' It was a friendly letter; she sounded like a nice person and that softened the blow somewhat. If Dad had been married to a lovely woman, surely it meant he must have been nice himself?

I sat down to reply straight away, telling her about Dad's remarkable resemblance to my husband Eric and filling her in about some of the details of my own life: my work, my children, my love of animals. We began a long, friendly correspondence and I invited her to visit us in Canterbury, but she said she was elderly and didn't like to travel much. She asked a lot of questions about my children, particularly about Helen's dancing – she had appeared in pantomime at the Marlowe Theatre in Canterbury for eleven years running and I was always backstage helping with make-up, costume changes and last-minute scenery malfunctions; she had also just been accepted for Elmhurst, a prestigious dance school where she would complete the last two years of her education while doing intensive ballet training. Dora seemed very impressed by that. She sounded like a very warm, naturally friendly person and it was lovely to make contact with her. She made me feel accepted as a part of her extended family and I was very glad I'd got in touch.

8

Losing My Real Father

Once Pop and Billie arrived in Scarborough, his health declined very quickly. Eric and I took the kids up on the train, doing a round trip to see Eric's family then on to Scarborough to see Pop. He'd got a mobility scooter and used it to play with the kids, but his recent memory was shot to pieces and he was frequently in a foul mood (which I learned is a common side effect of dementia).

Of course, I had to make a tentative peace with Billie in order to visit him once they were in Scarborough, but it was still difficult being in the house with her. I constantly had to button my lip and remind myself to be on best behaviour because the minute I walked in the door she wound me up and made me feel like a moody teenager again. Pop always seemed pleased to see me but sometimes he couldn't remember the names of the two grandchildren he used to dote upon, and I doubt if he'd have remembered mine if I hadn't always made a point of repeating it when I arrived.

'Hi, Pop! Your daughter Cherry has made it at last. How're you doing?'

His memory was better when we talked about the distant past: his work at Boscombe Down, the ponds he liked to dig in our gardens, and Mum – he often talked fondly about his Dorrie, as he always called her (short for Dorothy).

Billie was disabled, with rheumatoid arthritis affecting her knees, hips, spine and hands, and by 1982 they were dependent on regular visits from carers who made their meals, washed and dressed them. I tried to help when I was there, but Billie was as critical as ever, telling me I hadn't added enough salt, or that a dish was flavourless, or the food was too hot or too cold. Some things never change. I had to put up with it in order to spend time with Pop, so I bit my lip and smiled through gritted teeth.

For the final months of Pop's life, in the autumn of 1982, he was admitted to hospital and I popped up as often as I could, staying overnight at their house with Billie. By now, she slept in a special orthopaedic bed in the front room so I slept in their room, with their belongings scattered around, which felt very odd. There were two single beds – they'd been in single beds since West

Lavington, and in a rare candid moment, Billie told me that after they'd been married a few months she'd told Pop, 'That's it! No more sex.'

I saw Pop at hospital visiting times then came back to sit and watch telly with her during the evening, and frankly I couldn't wait until it was time to head home again. Staying there felt like stepping back in time – except my lovely Pop was no longer the person he had been back then because there was a blank expression in his eyes and he no longer spoke very much.

Pop started succumbing to chest infections and each time I would rush up to Scarborough only for him to pull through; he was a tough old bird. Helen was at dance school, while Graham had his O Levels coming up, so they couldn't join me. Pop had no quality of life left and he was suffering from a range of horrible conditions of old age, with all the attendant lack of dignity involved in having nurses perform intimate procedures on him. After he caught a chest infection for the third time the matron asked if I wanted them to continue with antibiotic treatment, and I made the decision not to.

I was staying at Billie's just a couple of days later when I took a telephone call to say Pop had died at ten past midnight. Right away I was determined to get to the hospital and spend some final moments with him, but I had a nightmare trying to find a taxi at that time of night.

When I finally got there I just sat by his bed, watching his features tighten and his skin colour blanche.

'I love you, Pop,' I whispered, 'I hope you are with Mum now. I'm going to miss you so much.'

He'd been a lovely father, a genuinely good man. Maybe it's strange that I wasn't more devastated by the loss, but after Mum's death, nothing could ever be so bad again. Besides, I'd had time to get used to Pop's decline. Once you've witnessed the final stages of dementia, you would never wish anyone you cared about to stay alive in that state. Perhaps I was bottling up my grief, as I had always buttoned up emotions since I was nine years old, but I felt quite calm as I got on with the business of arranging the funeral and sorting out the legal aspects of Pop's estate.

Helen desperately wanted to come up to Scarborough for her grandpa's funeral, but her dance school wouldn't let her catch the train without a chaperone, I didn't have time to go all the way down to Surrey to fetch her, and there was no one else willing to help. It was sad that she missed it, but it was a small funeral, since Pop and Billie hadn't been in Scarborough for long, they were both pretty old by the time they moved there and, besides, Billie had a habit of falling out with neighbours wherever they went. She managed to hobble in on her crutches and we gave him a decent send-off.

Driving back down the motorway afterwards to a love-less marriage and two children who were halfway out the door, I felt totally alone. Helen and I took the urn with Pop's ashes and had them buried in Mum's grave, and I looked at that mound, conscious that I'd lost the two people who had cared most about me in the world.

9

My Half-sister Sue

While I was still tied up with sorting out Pop's estate, Dora wrote, giving me the addresses of my father's sister Ada and my half-sister Sue. I read her letter with a start, feeling irrational guilt that I had contacted them while Pop was still alive. But it hadn't done any harm, and my curiosity was too great, so I sat down to write letters to them, introducing myself and saying that I looked forward to getting to know them. The weeks went by but I never received a reply from Ada; Dora had told me they were just on Christmas card terms and hadn't seen each other in many years, so I suppose she simply wasn't one for writing letters – or perhaps she was just too old by this time.

When Sue finally wrote back on a flowery notecard she seemed nervous, and told me she didn't know what to say. It was just general chit-chat at first, but then she told me something I hadn't heard about from Dora: that my birth father had won a Carnegie Medal for bravery (or 'heroic endeavour to save human life at risk to his own', as the award put it). During the night, two cars had crashed outside his house and burst into flames. Dad ran out in his pyjamas and dressing gown and managed to drag the drivers and passengers of both cars to safety, despite getting burned himself. A police inspector who lived up the road had recommended him for the award, which, Sue told me, she still had hanging in her hall. I felt a warm glow of pride at the knowledge that my birth father had been so courageous. The more I heard about him, the more I was sure I would have liked him. Wasn't I lucky to have had two wonderful fathers – the one I knew and the one I didn't?

Dora and I were corresponding regularly at this stage, but I heard less often from Sue and could tell that, like me, she had a very busy life. Then, early in 1983, a letter arrived asking if I would like to visit her and her husband. I jumped at the chance to meet my half-sister.

It was just after my fortieth birthday when I drove to Devon to meet Sue and her husband John. We'd already exchanged photos so I knew she was dark-haired and that there was a certain physical resemblance between us, and I recognised her straight away when she opened the front door. She and John were very lively and chatty and made me feel welcome from the start. I didn't get to meet their children, but Sue said, 'We'll have to introduce them to their new auntie next time you come down'.

It was just before dinner-time so I joined her in the kitchen to help as she cooked a meal for us. They had an open-plan kitchen, and John was sitting through in the adjoining room when he remarked, chuckling, 'I see you've both got the Noël arse!' Sue and I looked at each other and laughed: we had very similar figures, both of us wide-hipped and small on top.

After a lovely dinner, we went to the local pub just round the corner, and John showed me the butcher's shop where he worked. The conversation flowed quite easily: John chatted about the boat he'd just bought and told me I must come back in the summer when they'd have it out on the water. Sue told me that they made their own home-made wine and apologised that they didn't have a batch ready, or she would have given me a bottle to take home with me. We swapped stories about our children and our jobs, but there was nothing in depth. Most of the conversation was about the present and we said little about the past. Sue told me a few odd things about my father: that he had liked pickled onions so much that when her mum made them for him he often dipped into the jar and ate them before they'd had time to pickle much! She said that during the war he had been a gunner in the Royal Artillery. And he had been a smoker, like many men of his generation, and had succumbed to lung cancer at the age of sixty-three. He sounded like a kind, fun father. You hoped to keep your parents longer than that. We talked a little about losing our mothers so young, but didn't linger on the topic because we didn't want to drag down the mood of the evening.

There were loads of questions I wanted to ask: Why had Henri and my birth mother split up? Why did he not want me? Did he ever talk about my mother, Daisy? But I simply didn't ask. It takes time to get to know a person and you have to let relationships develop naturally. Besides, once you've been scarred by a death, as I had been by Mum's back in 1952, you find it hard to form new bonds because there's always a fear that this person might die as well. At least, that's what I was feeling at the time. I didn't tell Sue anything about what was really going on in my life: that I was married to a man I didn't love, but too scared to take any steps to end the marriage. We just chatted like two people who'd met on holiday, covering the broad outlines but nothing deeply personal.

I stayed overnight in their spare room then said goodbye after breakfast the next morning and drove back to Canterbury, mulling over the meeting. In my heart, I'd hoped there would be an instant connection, that Sue would feel like a long-lost sister and she would become an integral part of my life from then on. Instead, we'd been two polite and friendly strangers making conversation and I hadn't felt any particular bond. I blamed myself: it's because my emotions were so closed off that I couldn't react emotionally to meeting my half-sister. Maybe that was the problem with my marriage as well. Eric had never had a chance of winning my heart because I'd locked it up and thrown away the key before I met him.

I stayed in touch with Sue and Dora for a while, but just by letter and Christmas card. Then I received a letter from Sue saying she and John were planning to move to a tiny village in North Devon, but she didn't give me the address. After a period of time that felt longer than the normal gap between our letters, I wrote to Dora asking for Sue's new address so I could send a housewarming card, but there was no reply. Dora had always been a good correspondent before so I wondered if perhaps she had passed away and Sue hadn't had time to let me know, what with all the stress of the funeral and then moving house.

I wrote several times, both to the last address, with a note saying 'Please forward' on the envelope, and simply to her name, care of the village, North Devon, but there was no reply. It's not as if it was just down the road, but the silence bothered me, so one day I jumped in the car and drove there.

The village was basically one long road with houses set beside it, looking out over fields towards the River

Torridge. I parked at one end of the road and walked along, enjoying the peace and quiet. The lovely old stone houses were surrounded by greenery in all directions. I subtly glanced through windows, looking for a face I recognised, but there was hardly a soul in sight. I stopped in the village store to buy a drink and asked the shop-keeper if she knew Sue and John, but she said she didn't. My heart sank. Perhaps they hadn't moved here after all. I'd built up my hopes of finding them that day. In my head I'd pictured Sue apologising for the silence, perhaps explaining that she had lost my address in the move. And then I imagined us all hugging and going to the pub for a drink and a catch-up. It seemed that was not to be.

I didn't blame her at all; it was completely my own fault that I had lost contact with her, even though she was the only blood relative I had, the only member of my birth family I'd ever met. My hopes of finding a new family were dashed. Basically, I felt I'd blown it.

10

On the Trail in Jersey

I would have liked to go on foreign holidays sometimes but Eric said, 'I did all that travelling lark when I did my National Service.' Instead, we tended to go on boating holidays to the Broads or the Fens, or on a canal boat on the Thames near Guildford, with his brother Bernard and his wife Peggy. It wasn't an ideal holiday when the children were younger because they were stuck on the boat all day long without much to do, but we'd swim or go for walks, pick blackberries or go on an outing to the shops to buy food for the evening meal, and somehow we managed to keep them entertained. The men liked to moor in the middle of nowhere and fish at night, and Peggy and I would take the kids off in the dinghy to the nearest pub we could find.

However, after Pop died and I heard that Henri Le Gresley Noël had passed away, I found myself thinking more and more about Daisy Banks, my birth mother, and in the late summer of 1983 I asked Eric if we could go over to Jersey for a few days to poke around and see if we could come up with any more information about her.

I'd tried to track down Daisy Banks in the same way I'd found my father, but her name was so much more common that I'd had no success. Maybe if I actually went to Jersey I would find something, I reasoned. I might even come across someone who knew her. I think the detective element of the search for my family intrigued Eric; of course, he could approach it dispassionately, like a mystery to be solved, because it wasn't his family. For me, it had the potential to bring me into contact with my birth mother, and in the year my father had died that was bound to be very emotional.

We caught the train to Weymouth to take a ferry across to Jersey. I've always loved boats and I believe when you're going to an island, the correct way to approach is by the sea. If you fly in, you could be anywhere in the world, but sailing gives you the geographical context. It was a clear, sunny day and I stood out on deck for most of the four-hour crossing, watching big container ships go by on the horizon and the sun sparkling on the water. I felt very strange as I watched the shore coming into view: a greenish-brown rugged coastline with the occasional strip of beige sand and then a fort sitting on a rock just offshore, the Elizabeth Castle that dominates the town of St Helier. This was my homeland – or, at least, the homeland of my birth family. I wondered if I might pass someone in the street who was related to me without even realising it.

We came ashore in a port full of small sailing boats, with their sails fluttering in the breeze, and fisherman mending nets by the harbour wall. We'd booked into a little hotel near the front, and as we walked up there to check in I noted all the signs were in both French and English and you could hear both languages being spoken. It was clearly a halfway point between the two nations, and it had a distinctly foreign feel to it.

Our first stop on the search for my family was the library a few streets back from the waterfront. A librarian showed us the files of local newspapers going back decades, explaining that lots were missing, particularly issues that were destroyed during the war years. We sat down and worked through chronologically, checking the birth, wedding and death announcements in particular, and looking for any name that might possibly be a family one. It was a long, laborious process, real needle-in-a-haystack stuff.

Suddenly, my eye was caught by an obituary for a woman called Louisa Mary Renouf Banks, who had died in May 1975, eight years earlier. She'd been eighty-one years old, which made her a bit too old to be an aunt of mine, but perhaps she could have been my grandmother. It was pure chance, but it seemed as though the fates meant me to find this one.

The obituary notice mentioned the name of the firm of funeral directors who had arranged her funeral. 'We'll go there next,' Eric decided. There had been no other promising leads on people with the surname 'Banks' for several decades back, although we did wonder if William Louis Banks, who died in 1953, might be my grandfather.

Nothing would do but we were rushing across town to the funeral directors' office. Eric shot off ahead of me, and by the time I got there he was chatting to the owner, a little grey-haired man, about our search.

'Do you still keep records for 1975?' I asked.

'Oh yes,' he said. 'Of course we do. I'll just dig them out.'

He disappeared into a back office and re-emerged with a file, from which he pulled some papers then shuffled through them.

'Perhaps this will help you,' the man said, and he passed me a list of the mourners who'd attended Louisa Banks's funeral. There were only about ten of them and the name Renouf cropped up frequently – Bernard Renouf, Jean Renouf, Phyllis and Fred Renouf – but I couldn't see any more members of the Banks family. It sounded as though Renouf had been her maiden name.

'Do you have any contact details for the Renoufs?' Eric asked.

The man pursed his lips. 'I'm not allowed to give out names and addresses, but you should find them easily enough by checking in the phone book. Jersey's a small place, after all.'

We thanked him for his trouble and went back out to the street, where hazy sunshine was glinting off windows and warming the cobblestones.

'If we head back to the library, we can check the phone book there,' Eric said, about to charge off down the street. This meant nothing to him except a challenge at which he wanted to succeed, I felt. He had a competitiveness, perhaps from his football days, but he was blind to the fact that this was my family, my background, and I didn't have anyone else.

Suddenly, I felt a terrible weariness. I needed time to take all this in. I'd been on my own for so long that I felt overwhelmed by the thought that I might be about to meet a whole new family. I just wanted to sit and absorb the news. Besides, it could still be a false trail. Louisa Mary Renouf Banks might be someone else entirely. The Renoufs might have nothing to do with me.

I managed to persuade Eric to sit down and have a coffee, but as soon as we'd finished he was itching to go and it was back across town to the library to look up the phone book. Sure enough, there were lots of Renoufs in the St Helier area, including Phyllis and Fred Renouf, two names that had been listed among the mourners. We carefully wrote down their address and phone number then checked a map to find that it was just on the outskirts of town, not too far away.

'Shouldn't we telephone first?' I asked. It seemed a bit of an imposition to simply ring the doorbell, especially if they were elderly. They might be alarmed, thinking we were trying to rob them.

Eric was keen to go, though: 'It would be too difficult to explain on the telephone. If we turn up, they might recognise you if you have a family resemblance. Come on, Cherry. We've come this far; we've got to see it through.'

Reluctantly, I trailed along behind him as he walked at breakneck speed across town with the piece of paper in his pocket bearing the address of Phyllis and Fred Renouf. We arrived there to find it was a flat above a shop, and Eric rang the bell without any hesitation.

When an elderly man answered the door, Eric was ready with his opening line. 'I wonder if you know a lady called Daisy Louise Banks? My wife here,' he indicated me, 'is her daughter, who was given up for adoption, and she's trying to get in contact.'

The old man looked at me with interest: 'You're Daisy's girl, are you? Well, you'd better come on in, then.'

11

Tea with
the Renoufs

My heart was in my mouth as we climbed the stairs to their flat and the old man, clearly Fred, called out, 'Phyllis? One of Daisy's girls is here, asking after her.'

One of Daisy's girls: I immediately picked up on the phrase. That meant there was at least one more.

'Sit down and I'll fetch some tea,' Phyllis told us after bustling into the room to shake hands. She had short white hair, neatly set in a curly perm, and was wearing an old-fashioned flowery dress. Fred was in beige trousers and a hand-knitted pullover. I examined his features but couldn't discern any family likeness between him and me.

It was a large flat with a comfortably furnished sitting room. The windows looked out onto a leafy square with a statue in the middle.

As soon as we were seated on a chintz sofa, Eric started explaining: 'We found your names because you were in the list of mourners at the funeral of Louisa Mary Renouf Banks back in 1975. Was she a relative of yours?'

'Oh yes, she was my aunt,' Fred told us. 'The sister of my father, Bill Renouf.'

'And was Daisy Louise Banks related to them?'

'Indeed she was. Daisy was Louisa's daughter.' He looked at me and smiled. 'I suppose that makes us cousins of sorts, once or twice removed. I'm never sure how these things work.'

'Yes, I suppose we're distant cousins.' I smiled back, so nervous I hardly trusted myself to speak. This man might have the power to put me in touch with my birth mother. To me it felt cataclysmic, but everyone else in the room could have been talking about the weather; their tone was casual and everyday.

Phyllis came in with a tray of tea and biscuits, and we all busied ourselves with stirring in milk and sugar before getting back to the subject at hand.

'What a shame Bernard is away,' Phyllis remarked. 'He is Daisy's surviving brother – your uncle, I suppose. And she has a sister, Joyce, as well, who lives on the mainland. Bernard grew up alongside Sheila, your mother's oldest daughter, after Daisy, Joyce and Bill left during the evacuation. Bill died in the war, though.'

All the unfamiliar names followed one after the other and I wasn't sure I was following this properly. 'Daisy had a daughter before me?'

Oh my God, I had a sister and it sounded as though she was called Sheila. Wasn't that incredible?

'Yes. She was very young when she had her – sixteen or seventeen, I think – so her mother, Louisa – that's your grandmother – agreed to bring up the child alongside her own two youngest. Bernard and Joyce were like brother and sister to Sheila, although they were really her uncle and aunt.'

I hugged myself, trying to take it in. *Sheila and Paulette, Paulette and Sheila.*

Phyllis had taken over the talking from her husband now and she was in full swing. 'When Daisy and Joyce decided to join the evacuation of the island in June 1940, Sheila was a toddler and … well, I suppose Daisy thought she was best off where she was, even with the Germans coming. So she left her little girl here with her grandparents for the duration of the war.'

I was still coming to terms with the fact that I had a sister, Sheila, and couldn't think about the news that Daisy had left her behind during the evacuation. I asked the question that was foremost in my mind: 'Where is Sheila now?'

Phyllis shook her head and looked at Fred, who was

similarly blank. 'That I don't know. We lost touch a while back. Bernard or Joyce might be able to help.'

Eric butted in: 'How about Daisy? Do you know where she might be?'

'It's been a while since we've heard from her, but I'm sure I've got an address somewhere. I'll look it out for you before you go.'

My heart leapt. If I managed to find Daisy, surely she would be able to tell me where Sheila was. *My sister.* The words felt magical. I had a sibling. *I had direct, proper family with the same blood as me.*

'We know that Cherry was born in High Wycombe,' Eric said, 'because it says so on her birth certificate. Is that where Daisy went when she was evacuated?'

'Well, I suppose so,' Fred nodded. 'Joyce and her Belgian husband, Paul VanHellen, lived there and Daisy went to stay for a while.

'Did she come back to Jersey after the war?' Eric asked.

Phyllis replied: 'Oh yes, she was shuttling backwards and forwards for a while. Took poor Sheila over to the mainland with her. The girl didn't want to go because all her friends were here, and the people she thought of as her parents, even though they were her grandparents.' She smiled at me. 'This must be confusing for you, my dear. So many new relatives to grapple with all at once!'

I'd hardly said a word since we arrived, and I have no idea what the expression on my face was like but inside I was in turmoil. Phyllis and Fred were very friendly and welcoming but they didn't feel like long-lost family members. There was no hugging, no tears of joy, just tea and chocolate digestives in front of their gas fire. Maybe I was being unrealistic in my expectations.

Suddenly, Phyllis asked: 'Would you like to see some photographs?'

'Oh, yes please.' I hoped that seeing some pictures would make it all feel real, and help me to sort out all the names in my head by giving them faces.

Phyllis got to her feet to retrieve a dusty leather photo album from a bookshelf. She sat down beside me on the sofa and opened the first pages. 'That's Fred's grandmother, who was French.'

It was an ancient, faded black-and-white photo of a hunched, white-haired old lady, looking suspiciously at the camera as if she didn't quite trust this new-fangled contraption.

Phyllis turned a page and pointed: 'This one shows William and Louisa together – they're your grandfather and grandmother.'

They were young in the picture, perhaps newly married, both with neatly combed hair and Sunday-best clothes. It was a formal portrait in sepia tones that had been taken in a studio by a professional photographer, whose name was embossed on the cardboard frame.

'Here you are: that's Joyce and Bernard, your aunt and uncle.' I peered at them, working out the connections in my head. *There were four siblings: Joyce, Daisy, Bernard and Bill. Sheila and I were Daisy's daughters. 'Sheila and I': I just loved saying those words.*

'I'm not sure if we've got one of Daisy.' She flicked through the pages. 'Although I suppose that must be her there.' She pointed to a tiny, almost indistinguishable figure in the foreground of a family group shot.

I stared at the photo but could hardly make out any detail. All the same, it was a thrilling moment: the first glimpse of my birth mother. She had dark hair and was sitting cross-legged at the front of the group, looking rather bored with proceedings.

'Are you sure she's still alive?' I asked. 'It's just that when I tracked down my father, I found he had passed away eight years earlier.'

Phyllis looked at Fred. 'It's a long time since we've heard from her, but I'm sure Joyce would have heard if anything had happened. And she would have let us know. Daisy's only in her sixties, after all. She was born in 1921, if I remember rightly.'

I did the sums in my head. That meant she was twenty-two when she had me. And she'd been born the year before Mum and Pop got married so she was much younger than them.

'Here, let me write down her address for you while I'm thinking about it,' Phyllis said. She fetched an address book, which was sitting by the telephone in the corner, then copied out an address onto the back of an old envelope and handed it across: Daisy Noël Banks, Walk House, Keighley, West Yorkshire. I took the paper carefully.

'Why do you call her Noël Banks?' I asked.

'It's a Jersey tradition,' Phyllis explained. 'When your husband dies, you stick your maiden name at the end of your name, after his. But, of course, Daisy got divorced so she probably doesn't use the Noël name any more. You could leave that off.'

I wondered if that meant my father's mother's maiden name was Noël and her father's surname was Le Gresley? Henri Le Gresley Noël had always seemed a cumbersome mouthful of a name to me, although I rather liked the rhythm of it.

I wrote out our address in Canterbury for Phyllis and Fred to pass on to my new uncle Bernard, then said, 'We mustn't take up any more of your time. You've been most kind.'

Eric looked surprised – he'd just helped himself to another cup of tea – but suddenly I was finding it all too much. I needed some air, and some quiet time to process the information I'd been given. The names were whirling round my head like dead leaves in an autumn wind. I stood up, forcing Eric to stand as well.

'Thank you so much for inviting us into your home, and for all you've told me about the family.' I wondered whether we should hug since we were related, albeit distantly, but Phyllis held out her hand to shake mine and Fred did the same, then led us down the stairs.

'It's been a great pleasure,' Phyllis said. 'Do come back next time you're on the island.'

'We will,' Eric promised, then followed me as I set off down the street, for once ahead of him.

12

A Disintegrating Marriage

On the way back to the hotel, my thoughts were racing with all the new information I'd learned: I had a sister, and it seemed as though my birth mother was still alive. I wondered if Sheila lived up north near Daisy? I could catch a train up there and introduce myself. Maybe I could even go next week. My face flushed at the thought: it was overwhelming and somehow terrifying as well. What if we didn't get on? What if they decided they didn't want to know me? I couldn't bear to be rejected by either of them.

'I don't know why you were in such a hurry to leave,' Eric said as he caught up with me. 'I thought you would want to get your aunt Joyce and uncle Bernard's addresses from them. And you hardly asked anything about Daisy. I got the impression they rather disapproved of her, didn't you?'

'I don't want to talk about it,' I said. 'Please … can we give it a rest for a while?'

He wouldn't leave the subject alone, though. 'We can go back to the Register Office and apply for Daisy's birth certificate now we've confirmed her mother's and father's names and a rough date of birth. We've just got time to get there before it closes at four.'

'Eric, will you leave me alone? We can go to the Register Office tomorrow. I need some peace and quiet.'

I managed to persuade him to walk back to the hotel and once he was settled, reading the newspaper in the lounge, I headed out for a stroll on my own in the dusk. I wandered along the seafront, where hotels were separated from the sandy beach by a pedestrian walkway. Many of them had 'Vacancy' signs hanging out front as we were right at the end of the summer season. Seagulls cried over the shushing of the waves and there was a chill in the air when the sun disappeared over the horizon.

I'll go back home and I'll write to Daisy, but I won't get my hopes up, I told myself. *She didn't want me once before, so who's to say she'll want me now.*

A girl I knew through work had traced her birth mother a few years earlier and had received a letter in reply to hers, saying that the woman had no interest in meeting her or even entering into a correspondence. She had a new family now who knew nothing about her earlier pregnancy, and she wanted it to stay that way. My friend was devastated and I had to prepare myself in case that happened to me. Daisy might not want to know. And if that were the case, she would probably refuse to put me in touch with Sheila.

On the other hand, having met Fred and Phyllis Renouf, I'd got the impression of a family that was perfectly friendly, if not necessarily very close. They had their secrets, like all families, but they hadn't seemed at all surprised to meet me so it was obviously not a taboo subject that Daisy had had another baby during the war. I just didn't know what to expect and I felt sick with the tension. I breathed deep lungfuls of sea air in order to calm myself down.

Over dinner, Eric was full of questions we should have asked, and he even suggested going back to visit the Renoufs again the following day, but I didn't feel we should impose on their time any more. I did agree that we could go to the Register Office the next day, although I wasn't sure why we needed her birth certificate now we had an address for Daisy. And I'd decided I wanted to go to the cemetery where my grandparents were buried, just to pay my respects. I asked Eric if I could please go on my own, because it was such a personal thing, and he agreed.

Straight after breakfast I set off, buying a little posy of red and white roses from a street seller. I had asked for directions at our hotel and found the cemetery without any difficulty. A caretaker at the main gate looked up his lists and directed me down a gravel path and there it was: a lichen-covered grey headstone with the name William Louis Banks carved into it. It was a strange feeling to think that I was a direct descendant of this person, whom I had never known.

'Hello, I'm Cherry,' I said in my head. 'I wish we had met.' I knew so little about him and Louisa that it was hard to form any sort of picture, but I imagined them as honest, hard-working folk. William had died when I was just ten – the year after my mum died – while Louisa had died when I was twenty-three, so we could have had a proper relationship had I found her earlier. It couldn't be helped.

I met Eric at the Register Office, which was in a pretty tree-lined square where the cafés had outdoor tables. A wedding had just taken place when we arrived, and the bride and groom were standing outside beaming while their friends showered them with confetti. *Good luck to you*, I thought grimly. I wasn't a big fan of the institution of marriage anymore.

We went inside and I filled out applications for the birth certificates of Louisa Mary Renouf Banks and Daisy Louise Banks, paying the fee requested in Jersey pounds. The man behind the counter explained that he was standing in for a colleague who was off sick, but he was pretty sure he could find what we wanted.

'Are you related?' he asked, and I explained they were my grandmother and mother.

'Come back at three-thirty,' the man said.

That gave us a day in which to be normal tourists wandering along the beach, visiting Elizabeth Castle and the Jersey War Tunnels, and strolling through the immaculately kept gardens that were dotted all over the town, full of colourful exotic blooms.

You could walk out to the castle at low tide, but the water was right up at high tide so we caught a little ferry across. Eric was immediately reading all about it from a free leaflet, telling me that the castle dated from the 1590s, that Sir Walter Raleigh had been governor of Jersey, that Charles II hid there during the English Civil War … I tuned out his voice and wandered round, soaking in the atmosphere. From the battlements I gazed out to sea, trying to imagine how Daisy and her two siblings felt as they waved goodbye to the island's shores in 1940, unsure when they would see their parents again, and in Daisy's case leaving behind her little girl. Was she sobbing? How could she have brought herself to do that?

Once he'd looked around the castle, Eric wanted to hurry on and see the war tunnels. They were built by forced labour during the wartime occupation, providing a place for the Germans to store munitions where they would be protected from British air raids. They've now been turned into a museum telling the story of the occupation, and I wandered around picturing my grandmother, grandfather, my uncle Bernard and my sister Sheila having their house searched by the Gestapo and living in fear of arrest. I learned that the occupying troops got first priority when available food was distributed, so islanders were often starving. There were photos of people queuing outside a grocer's shop. When salt ran out they had to use seawater to flavour their food, then when tea was in short supply they used a mixture of parsnip and sugar beet. There was no petrol, so farmers reverted to using horses and carts to move goods around. It must have been tough, and of course no one knew how long the war would last.

I was starving so we had a sandwhich for lunch in a café, then went back to the Register Office at three-thirty to find the man there had printed out copies of the certificates for us. The only new information Daisy's gave me was her date of birth: 31 October 1921, so that meant she had been eight years younger than my birth father, Henri Le Gresley. I put them carefully into my handbag, hoping they'd come in handy one day.

At dinner in the hotel that evening, Eric and I ate in silence. I looked round at the other diners, all engaged in lively conversation, and felt sad that I wasn't one of them, in the kind of marriage where you were companions for each other. We had so little in common that when we found ourselves alone there was nothing to talk about. At home the children were usually around so it was never quiet, but being away together served to highlight the vast distance between us.

Next morning, we caught an early boat back to Weymouth, and I stood on deck, watching the coastline recede, in a mirror image of our arrival. I'd found out a lot during the trip and had no regrets about coming. I just wished with all my heart I had gone with someone more sensitive to my feelings about the situation … basically, someone I loved.

Suddenly, I burst into floods of tears and couldn't stop crying. Eric was below deck in the lounge, so at least I didn't have to explain myself to anyone. To tell you the truth, I couldn't have explained why I was crying. I suppose it was partly for Pop, whom I missed terribly, but it was also because I felt so alone in the world. Everything in my life felt incredibly, overpoweringly sad. I was still sniffling when the coast of England came into sight, and I felt shaky all the way home.

13

Making a Move

On our return from Jersey I didn't write to Daisy straight away. I drafted a couple of letters then tore them up and eventually sent a purely factual note, the same kind of note I had sent to my father's last known address. *Are you Daisy Banks of Jersey? Because I think I might be your daughter.* That kind of thing. I posted it, and two days later watched for the postman to see if there would be a reply by return of post. But there wasn't. For a week, I watched the postman every morning without any joy. One afternoon several months later, when I had given up all hope of hearing from Daisy, I got home from a chiropody appointment to find my original letter sitting in the hall with the words 'Not known at this address' scrawled across the front. The envelope had been torn open so that someone could look inside to get my address, and I flushed to think that a stranger had read the very personal message.

Eric came into the hall and saw me looking at the envelope. He'd obviously examined it earlier. 'We can write to Phyllis and Fred Renouf next,' he suggested. 'They can give us Joyce and Bernard's addresses and you can ask them for a recent address for Daisy.'

'I suppose so,' I said, but without enthusiasm. I'm a great believer in fate and karma, and it seemed as if the message I was being given was that I wasn't meant to find Daisy. To be honest, I was so devastated and emotionally wrung out that I didn't have the wherewithal to write another letter that might lay me open to more pain. I had too much on my plate to think of taking on one more type of stress. I felt all alone in the world, and finding my birth mother could be the most wonderful thing ever, bringing support and stability, or it could be another huge blow if I met her and it didn't work out. Extremes of emotion scared me. It felt as though I would be overwhelmed if I opened up and started to think about my situation, so I closed that lid firmly shut for the time being and got on with bringing up my children, riding my horses and earning a living.

One thing did change over the next few months, though: I moved out of our bedroom and into the spare room. My ability to keep up the pretence that all was well in our marriage was fast dwindling.

One evening, while we were watching TV, Eric got up to turn the set off. 'We need to talk,' he said. 'It's not natural for men to sleep separately from their wives. It's unhealthy.'

'No, it's too late,' I whispered.

Helen was still at dance school and Graham had gone out with his friends, so there was no one to rescue me by putting in an appearance. Eric leaned over, questioning me about what was wrong. I knew I owed him an explanation but I couldn't express myself. I shrank back in a big armchair, trying to get so far into it that I would disappear.

'God, you're acting like a caged animal,' he exclaimed, and that's exactly what I felt like.

I simply didn't know what to say to Eric. He wasn't a bad person. He was just not the man for me, and his idea of men's and women's places in the household were at least a decade out of date. I sometimes felt like his house-keeper rather than his wife, and chiropody clients had often mistaken me for the au pair when they saw me on the stairs with our two kids because of the age difference between us.

When the children were young, I'd never have contem-plated divorce. In the sixties and seventies, it was still very rare in our social group, and those who did split up were whispered about behind their backs, as if there was something not quite right about them. I didn't want my children to be bullied at school for having divorced parents, and I knew we would all be worse off financially were I to make a move. But I couldn't contemplate living with him once the children were no longer around. I watched a lot of old couples in the practice and knew you had to have the foundation of a love that was solid and true in order to have the patience to care for each other in old age.

Helen passed her A Levels at Elmhurst ballet school then got work as a dancer at Pontins in North Wales – which was something of a baptism of fire, she told me, but good for the CV. Graham sat his A Levels in May 1986, and that was it. I'd got my children through their secondary education. Helen had left home, Graham would be on his way shortly, and I knew I needed to do the same.

There was no final straw that broke the camel's back. Eric was going off on a golfing holiday with some friends straight after Graham's exams, and I simply decided that I wouldn't be there when he got back. I planned to tell him to his face, but knowing that it is hard to say exactly what you mean in such conversations, I also wrote him a note saying that I was very sorry but I had been living a lie because I didn't love him and I could no longer stay in the marriage. I left it on the breakfast table for him and went upstairs to pack my personal belongings into six large bin bags, since I didn't have a suitcase. I took the bags out to my beat-up Subaru pick-up, and when I came back in to the kitchen Eric was sitting reading the note.

'What's this all about?' he asked, waving it in the air.

'I'm leaving you,' I said, timidly.

'You don't mean it,' was his first reaction. 'You'll be back within a week.'

'No, I won't.' My voice was tiny, almost a whisper. 'It's all in the note, Eric. I'm sorry but I can't go on living like this.'

There was nothing more I could say so I turned to carry my last bag out to the Subaru, scooping my little terrier Widdy under my arm.

'You owe me for half the telephone bill,' he shouted after me. I used the house telephone for contacting my chiropody clients as well as for personal calls, and since we kept our practice finances completely separate I had to pay him for use of the phone.

I had £54 in my purse, the only money I had to my name. I whirled round, emptied the purse onto the kitchen table, coins spilling onto the floor. 'There you are,' I said.

Eric looked astonished. I took the opportunity to turn and walk out of the house that had become like a prison to me.

I drove to the end of the road without looking back, grateful that there was petrol in the van because I didn't have a credit card or any way of filling it up if there hadn't been. And then I stopped because I had no idea where to go. I hadn't made any plans. For the first time in my life I was a totally free agent, and the idea was exhilarating and terrifying at the same time.

14

A Larger-than-life Character

I drove to the home of a horsey friend, Pauline, who took one look at my face and knew straight away what had happened. 'Have you done it?' she whooped. 'Oh, well done. Come in and have a drink.'

'I don't know where I'm going to stay. And I've got no money.'

'Well, you can stay here tonight and we'll ask around, see if anyone has a spare room.'

As soon as we started spreading the word, we got a call from my friend Marion, another of our horsey circle. She had just bought a house in Whitstable, a picturesque town on the Thames Estuary with green fields sloping down to the beach. She was looking for a lodger for her big attic room, which was lovely, with sloping eaves and a skylight window, so I said I would take it. The whole time I felt as if the world was very far away. Nothing seemed real. I was having an adventure but at any moment I would wake up and find it was a dream.

Marion had a dog called Scrappy, and he got on very well with Widdy: too well, in fact. When I came home one day Marion's fella told me, 'I found your dog and our dog stuck together on your pillow.' When dogs mate, it's almost inevitable that the bitch will get pregnant, and sure enough Widdy was soon showing the tell-tale signs. That was all I needed!

Meanwhile, Eric had come back from his golfing holiday and was constantly on the phone trying to persuade me to come back. Public opinion among his patients in Canterbury was firmly against me: how could I leave a decent man like Eric who hadn't done anything wrong? I swear there were people crossing to the other side of the street to avoid me, so I tried to stay well away from the Canterbury area; if I had a client to see, I'd sneak in and out like an undercover secret agent.

Two weeks after leaving, I went to a pub called the Fox and Goose just outside Sittingbourne with a friend called Mo. We were having a drink and a chat when a loud voice called, 'Hello, Mo!' and I looked round to see a big man with a cheeky grin and not much hair, wearing a grand-dad shirt and chinos.

'How're you doing, babe? Who's this you've got with you? Can I buy you ladies a drink?'

Mo introduced him as her friend John. He was clearly a man with a lot of presence, and as he put our drinks on the table and squeezed onto the bench seat beside me I decided I didn't mind him interrupting our conversation. He was very masculine, with big shoulders like a bull, and he seemed like a cheerful type as well.

I could tell from his accent that John was an Essex boy, and he told me he worked as a meat inspector for a super-market chain but that he also ran a burger van and had a market stall selling watches.

'You sound like a regular Del Boy,' I told him, referring to the dodgy market-trader character in *Only Fools and Horses*.

He laughed. 'Yeah, that's about the size of it. Hopefully I'm a bit smarter.'

A friend of mine had just left her husband for a much younger man, so that was very much the topic of the evening. Mo told John that I had just left my husband.

'So what about you?' he asked me. 'Have you got a toy boy waiting in the wings too?'

'Me? I've had it with men,' I said emphatically. 'I bloomin' hate them. I don't want anything more to do with them.'

John and Mo laughed at my vehemence, then he picked up my glass and asked, 'Shall I drink this myself, then?'

'No, I can accept a drink, thanks,' I said, snatching it back. 'But that's it. Once bitten, twice shy, and all that.'

While we were chatting, John told me he was a bit of a junk collector who often went to country-house auctions. This was an era when lots of families were selling the silver plate to help with the upkeep of the manorial pile, and it made a nice day out, he said. 'That sounds fun,' I replied, thinking I should give it a try. I'd left all my domestic goods behind with Eric and would have to buy new kitchenware and a dining set some time – not to mention a sofa and a bed, which were slightly more pressing since I was sleeping on a mattress on the floor at Marion's. All that didn't bear thinking about for now. I was still practising chiropody but money was tight.

When we said goodnight, I knew John and I had clicked. We had that indefinable thing called chemistry that you can't predict, can't manufacture: it's either there or it's not. I'd told him I was living at Marion's, and two days later I wasn't particularly surprised when the phone rang and it was John, asking if I'd like to come to an auction with him. Despite what I'd said in the pub about never having anything to do with men, I felt as excited as a teenager on a first date. I even asked Marion's advice about what to wear, and I am decidedly not the girly type in normal circumstances.

John picked me up in his beat-up brown Renault and we drove to a house in north Kent. First we looked round at all the goods up for auction, and he decided that he had his eye on a set of china with some pheasants and deer painted on them. We stood in a crowded room as the lots were sold one by one. I'd been to horse auctions before and was always mystified by the secret language of nods and hand signs with which people committed themselves to purchases worth thousands of pounds. Sure enough, John seemed to be in on those secrets. I watched him while bidding was taking place for the china and, even standing right next to him, I could barely tell he was taking part. I felt like nudging him in the ribs in case he'd forgotten, but was worried my nudge might be taken as a bid.

'Sold!' cried the auctioneer, banging his gavel.

'Did you get it?' I asked.

'Sure did, babe!' he grinned and put his arm round me to give me a squeeze. It felt good.

'The trick is to walk away now, so I'm not tempted by anything else,' he said. 'Let's go and have a look round the grounds.'

There were lovely gardens outside but the ground was wet and John was wearing posh shoes. 'Don't matter,' he said, when I pointed out that they might get muddy. I'd soon learn that he took that kind of laid-back attitude to most things in life. 'Don't matter' was something he said often.

We walked and talked and told each other our potted life stories: it turned out we were exactly the same age and had been born within nine days of each other; he had grown up on Canvey Island and was still very close to his mum and dad; his mum had been a true Cockney, born in Bow, and as a result John had a nice line in Cockney rhyming slang ('Rosie Lee' being 'cup of tea' and so forth).

'I used to be a wrestler. My fight name was The Battling Butcher,' he grinned.

'Why that name?' It sounded a bit violent to me.

'I was a retchtub. Went into the family business as soon as I left school.'

'A retchtub?' I was beginning to feel really dumb, as if I should be understanding all this but had a mental block.

'It's butcher's back slang. You say words backwards. Keep up, Cherry!'

He told me he'd got married to a girl who worked in one of his dad's shops, and they'd had two daughters, Sam and Emma, who were in their teens, but his marriage had failed and he was on his own now. He was renting a place because his wife was still in the family home in Maidstone. The way he talked, I could tell he was a genuine character with a terrific sense of humour. Unlike poor Pop, he was clearly a glass half-full type. We had our first kiss out there in the gardens, under a big oak tree, and it felt completely right. He was like a big teddy bear; I knew I was completely safe in his arms.

On our second date, not long afterwards, John and I went for a walk, ending up in a country pub. He seemed nervous about something, and after much coaxing he confessed to me: 'I think you should know that I can't read. I know my letters and I can write words if someone spells them out for me, but I can't read back what I've written. If that bothers you, I'll fully understand if you don't want to carry on seeing me.'

My heart melted on the spot. 'That must have been really hard for you. But I can't see that it makes any difference to us, does it?'

'No, I suppose not. It's just that I'm used to being teased about it. Lots of people make fun of me. I need help reading letters and filling out forms. Even menus in restaurants can be tricky. Usually I say, "I'll have the steak, please," or I just point at something and see what arrives.'

It was strange seeing him so humble because up to now he'd seemed so full of confidence. 'It's a shame for you but it doesn't make one jot of difference to me,' I told him. I was pleased he'd told me because it showed he planned on sticking around, and I already knew that was what I wanted.

Before long, John had moved into Marion's attic room with me, where we both slept on the mattress on the floor. He was there to help me the night Widdy went into labour and produced her pups. You know for sure you've got a decent bloke when he helps you to clean up afterbirth. He added his own suitcases to all the chaos of a bitch and her suckling pups, amidst my boxes of possessions spilling out their contents across the floor.

When two people come together in their early forties with failed marriages behind them, there are always umpteen complications. I would have to hire a lawyer to institute divorce proceedings, which I knew Eric would resist, and John had his own legal proceedings going on over custody of his daughters. I was still commuting back to the Canterbury area to do home visits as a chiropodist, because it was the only way I could earn decent money, but I was finding it increasingly stressful. I felt responsible for these old souls I visited, especially the ones who didn't see another human being all day long, and I'd often find myself popping in to check they had turned off their electric blankets, or that the dinner hadn't burned in the gas oven. And on top of all that, I became stepmother to John's two daughters. When I first met Sam and Emma, I had my own experiences with Billie at the forefront of my mind, and I was determined not to make all the mistakes she had in the way I related to them.

'I had a wicked stepmother,' I told them, 'so I know what that's like. But I'm not going to be a mother to you. If I can, I'd like to be your friend.'

They were sweet girls, who seemed to enjoy spending time with us. I knew it must be a very unsettling time for them, and I tried my best to tread lightly while I got to know them.

A few months after I'd left, Eric was still phoning fairly regularly over one thing or another, so I wasn't surprised to hear his voice when I picked up the phone one evening.

'You'll never guess who I've just been talking to,' he said, and something in his tone made me prick up my ears.

'No. Who?'

'Someone you've been trying to find for ages.'

'Just tell me who it is, Eric.'

'Daisy Banks. Your mother. We had a long chat and she wants to hear from you.'

For thirty seconds I stopped breathing. I was so thrown by his answer that I didn't think to ask how he'd got her number or what he'd told her about me. He'd found my mother, and what's more she wanted to hear from me. It was the most wonderful news in the world!

15

Getting in Touch
with Daisy

After I hung up I sat staring at Daisy's telephone number, scribbled on the pad by the phone. John came out into the hall.

'Was that Eric again?' he asked, and his mouth fell open when I told him what the call had been about. 'Blimey. You going to give her a ring, then?'

'First I need to think about what I'm going to say.'

'You can't really plan these conversations, babe. You'll just have to call up, introduce yourself then go with the flow.' He gave me a kiss on the forehead. 'Do you want me to sit beside you and hold your hand while you make the call?'

'I don't think I can. I'm not ready.'

'Just dial,' he urged. 'The more you think about it, the harder it will get.'

He was right. I picked up the phone and dialled the number, my hand shaking. It rang and rang, and I decided I would hang up after ten rings, but then the ringing stopped and I heard a voice saying, 'Hello?'

'Hello,' I replied. 'I'm Paulette.' Mum once told me I'd been named after Paulette Goddard, the actress who often starred in Charlie Chaplin films. This woman, Daisy, must have chosen the name for me, since that's what is written on my birth certificate and she's the one who registered the birth. What an odd thought.

'I'm *so* happy to hear from you, Paulette.' She sounded close to tears. 'I can't believe it's you after all these years. I had a long chat with your husband earlier. Did he tell you? It sounds as though he really cares about you, so I'm sorry to hear you two have split up.'

'Believe me, it's for the best,' I told her. 'It's been a long time coming. I married for all the wrong reasons and stayed with him just until the kids were independent.'

'He said you live in Kent. Are you still there?'

'Yes, I am. Where are you?'

'I've just moved into an old people's bungalow in Leeds. It's a bit small but there are wardens who will come if I press my alarm button. I have health problems, you see. I'm rather frail.'

'I'm sorry to hear that.'

'Oh, I don't want to talk about my health. It's a long, boring story. I'm just so glad to be talking to you, my daughter Paulette. I want to hear all about *your* life.'

'Do you happen to know how Eric found you, by the way? He didn't mention it to me – he just said that he'd had a chat with you.'

Her answer was hesitant. 'I think Joyce must have given him my number. My sister Joyce, that is. He said you went over to Jersey and met Fred and Phyllis.'

I guessed that Eric must have contacted them after I left him. He hadn't wanted to leave the search unresolved when we left Jersey. 'Yes, that was three years ago. We went to Jersey hoping to find you. I'm glad it worked out in the end. There's so much I want to ask you.'

'Yes, me too. I hear I have grandchildren …'

I told her about Helen and Graham, about my work and why my marriage had ended, and then I told her about John, the new man in my life, and she said she was delighted to hear I was happy. 'Life's too short to be lonely,' she said. I thought she sounded lovely. So far she was asking the right questions and saying all the things I wanted to hear.

'I've been looking for you for ages,' I told her. 'You were really difficult to track down. I tried to get in touch with your ex-husband Henri Le Gresley Noël as well, but I'm sorry to say I had a letter from his wife telling me he died in 1974.'

'Dead, is he?' she said. 'He's the one that ran off with the Welshwoman. I haven't seen him since you were born.'

I explained that he had married someone called Lil and had a daughter, Sue, whom I had gone to stay with, and that after Lil died he had remarried, to her cousin Dora, who'd been very friendly to me.

'Married his wife's cousin, did he? So he had three marriages, like me.'

'You had three marriages?'

'That's right. My third husband, Pete, is still around.'

'There was another one in between Henri and Pete, was there?'

'Oh, it's a tragic story, Paulette. I'll tell you about it another time. It wouldn't be right in our first conversation.'

'Can we meet for a chat?' I asked. 'It would be lovely to see you face to face. I don't mind driving up your way.'

'Yes, we must do that,' she said. 'I'll have to get back to you about the best time, though, because I'm in the middle of some medical tests. To cut a long story short, I took an arthritis drug called Opren that caused some nasty side effects and I'm fighting for compensation. It means I have to keep going all over the place for tests the lawyers want me to have. It's taken over my life for now.

But we could write in the meantime. Why don't you give me your address?'

We swapped addresses, reading them back to each other to make sure there were no mistakes.

'I have to go now but I'll write soon,' Daisy promised.

'There was one more thing I wanted to ask,' I said quickly. 'Do I have a sister called Sheila?'

'Oh yes,' she said. 'Sheila. I'll put it all in a letter. Talk soon. Bye, Paulette. Lovely to speak to you.'

She hung up and I sat in the hall, clutching the phone while I took it all in, trying not to forget a single word.

John came out. 'How did it go?'

'Good,' I said. 'She sounds nice. She's going to write.'

I think he could tell that I was feeling a bit shaky because he came over to give me one of his teddy-bear hugs, the ones that made me feel safe, as if nothing or no one could hurt me ever again.

'Do you know something funny?' I said, squinting up at him. 'Her voice is just like mine. She doesn't have a Wiltshire accent, but we've got the same tone. Isn't that strange?'

'It's nice,' John said. 'You'll probably find lots of genetic similarities between you. Blood is blood, after all.'

It's hard to describe what it's like to contact your birth mother for the first time in your life. Maybe only those who've been through it will understand. First and foremost, I was curious to find out what kind of woman she was. I really wanted to like her, to discover that she was a good person who had only given me up for adoption because she had no other choice. I hoped that she was close to my sister Sheila, that she would introduce us and we would all end up being part of each other's lives. I was excited but at the same time there was a fear of rejection: I couldn't bear it if she decided she didn't want anything to do with me after all. It didn't sound as though that was likely from our conversation, but still I was wary.

It was that old conundrum: I tried not to let myself hope for too much so that I couldn't be hurt yet again – but at the same time I'm basically an optimistic person and I was keen to find out more, so I wrote to Daisy the very next day, sending a few photographs of me, Helen and Graham. I asked about Pete, and whether they'd had any more children. I had so many questions it was hard to stop once I started, but telling each other about our children seemed a good starting point.

Within a week I had a letter back from Daisy. '*Dear Paulette,*' it began, which felt odd to me, since no one used that name any more. She told me she had had four children with her current husband, Pete Barton: Sally, Lizzie, Marie (known to everyone as Mid) and Peter (the youngest). She said she'd already told them about me and they were all looking forward to meeting me. With my permission, she would give them my address so they could write to say hello. She then went on to praise my children, saying, '*Graham sounds a very hard-working boy*' (he'd done well in his A Levels and was now studying saddlery and leather goods at Cordwainers College in Hackney, London). '*Helen looks beautiful,*' she said, then told me that she used to be a dancer herself. She'd started at the age of twelve, and before the war she had toured the continent, winning medals for ballroom dancing. I couldn't wait to share this with Helen! It seemed there was a gene for dancing in our blood, but unfortunately it skipped a generation with me because I'm totally uncoordinated.

One of the photos I'd sent showed me with my horse, Copper, and Daisy wrote back that her dear father's life was horses – big beautiful shires – which he worked with as assistant veterinary surgeon to Jersey's vet. It was wonderful to think that my love of horses might have been passed down in the family, and I warmed to this man, my long-dead grandfather. Then came a shock: Daisy wrote that he had been imprisoned in a concentration camp during the war for being in the Resistance. When he came out he weighed five stone instead of fourteen; she added in brackets that he was six foot two inches tall. I'd seen the pictures of survivors of Auschwitz and

Belsen, but it was hard to imagine how a grown man could sink to a weight of just five stone and still be alive. It must have been horrendous for the family. I'd had no idea from the little I'd read that conditions were so harsh on the islands when they were under occupation. Daisy wrote that she'd never been able to talk about the war, telling me that her nineteen-year-old brother Bill had been killed by the Germans. The Renoufs had mentioned that in passing but I hadn't made the connection. I realised that on top of the anxiety about her father's fate and the grief about her brother's, she was living away from her family during the war, away from her little girl Sheila, and then she was forced to give me up for adoption. What she must have been going through was unimaginable. My heart went out to her.

I drank in every word of her letter, memorising each last detail. My grandmother had been a farmer's wife who had twenty children – *twenty!* – and spent her life doing washing and manual work, yet she still had beautiful hands. They kept having to move home and she piled all their belongings onto a handcart and wheeled it through the streets. I couldn't get enough information about my birth family. I wanted to know everything, all at once.

Daisy and I spoke on the phone again, and this time we were more relaxed with each other, chatting about our partners, my trouble keeping up with my work while looking after John's two daughters when they were with us and preparing for Christmas.

At the end of the call she suggested that maybe we could meet on Boxing Day, just a few weeks away, and I immediately leapt at the chance.

'I can't think of a Christmas present I would rather have,' I said, and I truly meant it.

16

The Boxing Day Meeting

While I'd been writing to my newly discovered birth mother and dealing with all the myriad emotions that entailed, there was drama in another part of our lives as well. John's legal battles with his ex-wife culminated in us being awarded custody of his two daughters, Sam and Emma, and moving back into their family home in Maidstone to look after the girls. My divorce from Eric had just come through, but the small lump sum I got from that was immediately swallowed up by the costs of buying out John's wife's share of the house. It was a difficult time for all concerned. Neither John nor I liked Maidstone, but we felt it was important in a time of upheaval that Emma didn't have to change schools (Sam had already left school and was working in a bakery) and that they stayed close to their friends. We had to try to give them peace and stability. I could well remember what it was like to have a new stepmother who uprooted the family to move to a place of her choosing, and I was determined not to do the same to them.

While I was trying to learn how to manage their household – what food the girls ate, their domestic habits, how they liked their jeans ironed – it was impossible for me to carry on with my chiropody work. I decided to give it up and look for what I called a 'zombie job', one that didn't require any intellectual or emotional energy. A contact of John's got me a job at the meat plant where he worked, a job in which I could just stand doing repetitive work all day and get paid for it.

All the while my thoughts were buzzing as I tried to picture the forthcoming meeting: how would Daisy and I get on? Funnily enough, I got a letter from her in early December showing that she was feeling just as anxious as I was. '*What if she doesn't like the look of me? What if she doesn't like my type of person?*' she wrote. It seemed we were both winding ourselves up into a bit of a state about it. I wrote back that my philosophy of life was just to be yourself, and if other people don't like you, that's their problem. Daisy replied that her philosophy was identical, and she was amazed at how similar we sounded. She was very loving in that letter, writing, '*The feeling of joy overwhelms me – just imagine, I can touch you, actually feel you again,*' and it just served to make me even more excited about our meeting.

I was curious about the Barton children, and I didn't have long to wait before they got in touch, one by one. '*Hello, I'm Sally,*' read a letter on bright green notepaper. '*Welcome to the family. It's lovely to think that I have another sister.*' She wrote that she was twenty-eight and for the past six years had been working in a nursing home for the terminally ill. What a tough job that must be! Her letter was chatty, telling me about the flat where she was staying and her plans for Christmas, and I thought she sounded absolutely lovely.

There was a very warm phone call from Lizzie and then a long letter from Pete, Daisy's son, the youngest family member, who told me he drove HGVs for a living. It was all sounding very positive and exciting, and then came a blow: a short note from Daisy arrived less than a week before Christmas saying she had to cancel the Boxing Day meeting because her husband had to work. To say I was devastated is an understatement. I just stared at the page in disbelief.

We'd already chosen a location – Bedford – simply because it would take Daisy roughly the same length of time to get there from Leeds as it would take us from our place in Maidstone. I'd arranged my whole Christmas so that I had my kids on Christmas Day and they went to their dad on Boxing Day. Helen had been off dancing with a company in Turkey and I was dying to spend as much time with her as I could on her return, but I had cleared Boxing Day in order to meet Daisy. Could it mean that she was chickening out of meeting me at all? I decided to phone her and see what the problem was.

'It's just that Pete Senior was going to drive me down,' she said, 'and I'm not sure if he's free.'

'I suppose we could come up to Leeds if that's what it takes,' I offered, mentally calculating how long the drive would take. Perhaps we'd have to stay overnight in a B&B.

'Tell you what, I'll talk to Pete again and see if he can change his plans. I've been so busy going to hospitals, I don't know where I'm at. I was down at a clinic in Harley Street last week having scans and blood tests, and Pete Senior took me to that.'

'I'd really like to see you if you can manage it …' I crossed my fingers.

'OK, well, I'm sure I can persuade Pete to change his work plans. Or maybe Pete Junior can bring me instead. Perhaps we should meet in Bedford on Boxing Day after all. Will we do that? Just stick to Plan A? I can't wait to see you.'

'That would suit me, if you can manage.' When I came off the phone I wondered if it was nerves that had caused the hiccup. I was nervous too, but bubbling with excitement at the same time.

Boxing Day morning was crisp and sunny, with a cloudless blue sky and silvery frost making the fields and hedgerows glisten. My stomach was churning but we chatted about the kids and listened to tapes. We were low on petrol and there were no garages open to top up. John was always the optimist, happy to drive on an empty tank, saying, 'There's plenty in reserve,' while I was chewed up with nerves, worrying that we wouldn't make it but would break down by a roadside somewhere. I suppose it served to distract me from worrying about meeting Daisy! On this occasion we got away with it and arrived in plenty of time, since the roads around London, usually a nightmare, were miraculously clear. John was driving but he kept his hand on my knee most of the way, a sign of reassurance that meant a lot to me.

We'd arranged to meet beside the statue of John Bunyan that stands at the top of Bedford's high street. The roads were empty as we approached, and when John drew up alongside the tall bronze statue, we couldn't see a woman anywhere. There was just an elderly man with silver hair on the sides of his head, bald as a coot on top. He looked up as we approached.

'Are you Paulette?' he asked.

John was on the driver's side and he said, 'Yes, she is.'

'I'm Pete Barton, Daisy's husband. She's in the car round the corner. She was too nervous to come down here herself.' He chuckled. 'But she's really looking forward to meeting you.'

We parked the car and I walked over to shake hands with him. I introduced John and they did a bit of male back-slapping, then I peered round and asked, 'Which way is the car?'

He pointed to a cross-street. 'Just over that way.'

John and I started walking, hand in hand, and I was glad of his physical presence because I was afraid my knees might give way at any time. My chest was tight and I had a rushing sound in my ears. I was wound up like a top.

When we were about ten feet away from the car, the door opened and an elderly woman climbed out, holding onto the doorframe for support. She was like a shorter version of me, dressed in brown crimplene trousers, a brown quilted jacket and a thick brown headscarf. I was dressed in reasonably fashionable eighties style, in a midi skirt, baggy pink jumper and cowboy boots.

'Daisy?' I asked, then we walked straight into each other's arms and had a big hug. All I could think was, 'Oh my God, this is my mother!'

'My, you're beautiful,' she said, peering at me through her glasses. 'I'm so happy. I can't believe this is finally happening.'

'Me neither. You've got no idea how much this means to me.' I pulled back to look at her face properly and saw there was definitely a family resemblance. We had the same nose and mouth, the same shape of face. She looked older than her sixty-five years, but the lines on her face were smile rather than frown lines and, like me, she had tears in her eyes. I pulled a tissue from my handbag and offered it to her then got out another one for myself.

As soon as that initial hug was out of the way, I didn't feel so shaky any more. She seemed pleased to see me; the difficult bit was out of the way. John shook hands with Daisy then I noticed a young man with dark hair, a beard and glasses was hanging back, waiting to get our attention.

'I'm Daisy's son,' he said. 'Pete Junior. Nice to meet you, big sis!' He gave me a hug, grinning from ear to ear.

John shook hands with him then Pete Junior suggested, 'Shall we go to the pub? I saw one just down the road.'

A drink was exactly what I needed. We trotted off to the pub, chatting about neutral things like the lack of traffic on the way there, and how we had spent our respective Christmas Days.

We commandeered a corner table in the pub and John and I ordered gin and tonics while Daisy had a glass of wine and the two Petes had a pint each. It was quite busy and the atmosphere wasn't conducive to very personal chats, but soon we were all laughing and joking, the men sharing anecdotes about their work and Daisy and I chatting about our children. She showed me photos of my half-sisters, the ones she'd had with Pete, and they all looked like nice, friendly women. Pete Junior filled me in a bit on their jobs, their partners and their personalities, while I concentrated hard, trying to memorise names and faces. His own wife was called Anne, he told me, and they had two young boys.

'What about Sheila?' I asked. 'You haven't shown me a picture of her. Do you see much of her? Where does she live? I'd really like to meet her.'

Daisy made a tutting sound.

I stared, waiting for her to say something. It seemed as though there had been some kind of falling out, but I didn't feel as though I should pry. Instead of explaining, Daisy asked, 'When can I meet Graham and Helen? I'd love to meet my new grandchildren.'

'You'll have to be quick if you want to see Helen because she's back off to Turkey in a few days. Maybe you could come down and stay with us in Maidstone next time she's over.'

'Oh, I'd love that,' she said. 'And I could meet your lovely stepdaughters as well.' She reached out and squeezed my hand. 'Isn't this wonderful? I still can't believe we're here, together. I've dreamed of this moment for so many years – ever since I lost you, in fact.'

The pub kitchen was about to close so we ordered lunch. Daisy fumbled with her glasses, switching to another pair to read the menu.

'Damn Yanks!' she said. 'I didn't even need reading glasses until I took that stupid drug of theirs. Now my eyesight's shot to pieces and I get rashes if I go out in sunlight. You take what the doctor prescribes for you without question and look where it gets you!'

'Are there many other people with the same problems from that drug?' John asked.

'There are thousands of us and we all have to be individually assessed. They've got me jumping through hoops like you wouldn't believe. But at least I should get a big pay-out at the end of it all.'

'Yeah, we want to buy a cottage by the sea,' Pete Senior said.

Daisy grinned. 'We'll get a big place so you can all come and visit.'

After we had finished eating, Pete Junior pulled out a camera to take snaps of us all. We put our arms round each other and grinned while he took some inside the pub, then John took the camera so that Pete could be in a photo with his 'new sister'. Next, Daisy spotted a Rolls-Royce in the car park outside, and nothing would do but she and I posed beside it, pretending it was ours, while Pete Junior took photos.

The light was starting to fade by three o'clock, and Pete Senior said, 'We'll have to get up the road soon, Daisy, old girl.'

I didn't want her to go yet. 'There's so much I haven't asked you … About what happened when I was born, and your second husband, and Sheila … I don't even know where to start.'

'Tell you what, I'm going to write down the story of my life for you,' she promised, clutching my hand and squeezing it tightly. 'It will be easier for me to tell you that way. I'll get onto it straight away. Now, I hope you two have a safe journey home. You're lovely people and you've made an old woman very happy.'

There was a glint of tears in her eyes as we hugged goodbye and I kissed her cheek. 'I'll see you again very soon, won't I?' I asked, feeling teary myself.

'You bet,' she said, and grinned then blew me a kiss.

As we walked down the road to the car, John asked, 'You OK?'

'Yeah. It was all very chatty and relaxed, wasn't it? As if we've known them for ages. It didn't feel odd at all at the time, but it was actually one of the most peculiar experiences of my life.'

'Do you like her? Does she feel like a mum?'

124

I had to think about that. Daisy was not remotely like my mum who had died when I was nine, but she seemed affectionate and caring.

'Yes, I think I do like her,' I replied. 'But no, she doesn't feel like a mum.'

17

Daisy's Story

When I woke the next morning and memories of the meeting came flooding into my head, I had to blink to remind myself it wasn't a dream. I was forty-three years old and the day before I had met the woman who gave birth to me; what's more, it had gone well. There had been no awkward silences, just goodwill all round and a desire to get to know each other better. It hadn't been the right kind of atmosphere for me to ask the questions I really wanted answers to, but I hoped the letter containing her life story would come soon and then maybe we could arrange our next meeting. John was still asleep beside me and I snuggled up to his warm body, thinking how lucky I was that at last everything was turning out the way I wanted it: I had my own immediate family close to me and a big extended family just a phone call away.

Daisy called me later that day, just as I was about to call her. 'Great minds think alike,' I quipped. She wanted to make sure we'd got home safely and to ask if I would mind if she wrote to Graham and Helen and gave their addresses to their new siblings as well. The speed at which new connections were being made was slightly overwhelming, but of course I agreed.

'I can't tell you how much it meant to me to meet you,' Daisy said. 'It's been like a missing piece of a jigsaw puzzle in my life all this time. I didn't know where to start trying to look for you, but I always hoped you would come looking for me. I'm so grateful that you did.'

Two days later, the post brought further evidence of how emotional she was feeling. I received a letter, which she said was written at 2 a.m. the night after she left us, addressed to '*two of the dearest people I can think of … my beloved daughter and her fantastic man*'. She went on to say, '*as long as I live I will remember that first look at your beautiful little face … I could never put into words this feeling of love I have for you.*' She said she had been sobbing in the car on the way home and that now she had '*a feeling deep inside of me … of just pure unadulterated Mother love*'.

It was a lovely letter to receive, and I was gratified that she felt so strongly about me. I wrote back that our meeting had been very important for me too and I was glad we felt the same way about each other. Before we got in touch I'd felt as though I had my back to a brick wall; my kids and John were the future and they were in front of me, but there was nothing behind me. And now I'd begun to realise that there were windows in that brick wall and faces were beginning to come into view in these windows, giving me a past as well as a present and future.

Helen and Graham were fascinated to hear all the details of our meeting and were looking forward to being introduced to their new 'grandma', but after New Year it was back to work for all of us so that would have to wait. I applied for promotion to a slightly more interesting job as an ancilliary (in other words, a dogsbody) in the cutting room at the plant. To get the job I had to demonstrate to all the men there that I could push stainless steel bins loaded with meat up a slope onto the scales. Thirty butchers lined up to watch my test, shouting, 'Go on, girl! You can do it!' Somehow I managed by taking a run at it and using my body weight, and I got the job in the cutting room, which was just as boring as the last job but had the merit of being slightly better paid.

And then in mid-January I received a thick envelope in the post and opened it to find fourteen pages of handwriting on lined school-type paper. The heading on page one was 'Harold', which meant nothing to me, and on the last page it said *'This is not a letter, just documents'*. It was Daisy's story of her life, which she had written out for me in blue ink. I grabbed a coffee and curled up in a chair; cooking the dinner for everyone else could wait.

First of all, Daisy wrote that after she left me as a baby, she went back into the ATS – the Auxiliary Territorial Service, which was the women's corps in the army during the Second World War. I remembered one of the photos she had sent me showed her in ATS uniform. She wrote that after she had to give me up, she 'missed [her] baby girl madly', but consoled herself with the belief that the war would soon be over. And then, during her training, they went on a climb of Ben Nevis, and when she got down the mountain there was a stranger among the group who helped her with her kit, and who introduced himself as Harold Arthur. She confided in him about how much she wanted her child back; he was very sympathetic and soon they became an item. '*From that minute on, we were never apart*,' she wrote.

The war dragged on until '*Three years later we started our search for you but couldn't find you in High Wycombe or Uxbridge*'. Of course, by that time Mum, Pop and I had moved to Salisbury. But what made Daisy think she could come and claim me back from them after the war? She had signed the adoption papers and it must have been explained to her what they meant. I was puzzled. What would she have done if she'd found me? She didn't explain anywhere *why* she had given me up for adoption, but I assume it was because Henri Le Gresley had left her, her parents were stuck on Jersey under German occupation and she couldn't bring me up on her own. It was doubly understandable if it was true that her sister had thrown her out of the house after she called her brother-in-law a Kraut – but there was no mention of that incident I'd heard about from the Renoufs in Jersey.

Daisy wrote that after Jersey was liberated, she went back straight away on a Red Cross boat because she'd had word that her father was dying. She and Harold moved in to a flat above her mother and father's flat, and Sheila, her daughter, came and went between the two. Meanwhile, Daisy wrote, she continued the search for me, looking in London, Southampton, Kent (where Harold's family lived), but never in Wiltshire.

She and Harold got married at St Helier Register Office: I remembered the couple I'd seen coming out of there and wondered if it was still the same building. Then, Daisy continued, about six months later she noticed he was huddled over with pain. He claimed it was just lumbago, but she persuaded him to go to a doctor, who diagnosed a kidney problem and recommended that he fly back to Kent, since the hospital in Jersey did not have the facilities to treat his condition. She spoke to him on the telephone on the evening of his arrival in a hospital near Ashford, and he joked that he'd been placed in the maternity unit because his stomach was so swollen up. Then Daisy was at work the following morning when she took a phone call from someone at the hospital saying, '*I regret to inform you that your husband died at five this morning*'. She simply couldn't believe it at first, but an autopsy found he had died of amyloid disease, a rare but deadly condition. She was so shocked that she couldn't cry, and for a long time she couldn't speak to anyone but her daughter Sheila. She wrote, '*If there is an afterlife he will be waiting; a love like ours will never die*'.

It must have been desperately sad to be widowed when she was still only in her twenties. Her first husband had left her for a Welshwoman and her second had died after six months of marriage; poor Daisy was not having much luck with men.

She was in mourning for ages but eventually, Daisy wrote, she went back to work, training as a State Enrolled Assistant Nurse and living on Jersey. However, in 1949, when Sheila was twelve years old, she wrote '*as she was a very high IQ child, it was suggested that her education could be further advanced if she could attend a certain school in Southampton*'. Daisy took her over to Southampton, where she had a nursing job looking after a patient she had nursed at the General Hospital in Jersey, and enrolled her for the school that had been recommended.

While Daisy was sitting in a café opposite the school one day, waiting for Sheila to come out of an exam, a man walked up to her and introduced himself as Pete Barton.

'*Now, I have always been a pushover for people's eyes – yes, eyes, the mirror of the soul and all that. That man was desperately in need of someone to talk to and boy, did he talk!*' she wrote. '*One hour later this man had told me his life story,*' and she listened to him for ages before remembering that Sheila was standing all on her own, waiting for her over at the school.

While Sheila attended this special school in Southampton, Daisy was nursing a private patient – and whenever she was off duty Pete seemed to appear. She was planning to get the boat-train back to Jersey after Sheila passed her all-important exam, but Pete begged her to marry him so she went to the registry office and they were wed the very next morning. Pete got a job with the army at Catterick Camp in Yorkshire, and they moved to a cottage there. '*Sheila wouldn't come,*' Daisy wrote, but she went all the same and her daughter Susan was born a year later.

Susan? I was confused for a moment until I remembered her saying that Lizzie, the eldest of the children she had with Pete, had been called Susan at birth.

They seemed to have moved a lot, from Yorkshire to Ashford to Southampton to Rochdale, and all the time money was tight so Daisy took a range of jobs, at one time running a café, as well as having three more children. She wrote that she had worked as an NSPCC foster mother until the kids reached their teens, and I wondered how on earth she had managed that as well as raising four of her own. It all sounded like a desperate story of hardship and struggle. She must be a very resilient woman.

I put down the pages and took a slurp of my stone-cold coffee. It was such an odd story that I genuinely didn't know what to make of it. Daisy had told me about her relationships with her second and third husbands, but nothing about the first husband, Henri Le Gresley Noël, the one who was my father. She'd told me about her children with Pete Barton but very little about her daughter Sheila, who was my sister. Still, now that we were in touch I could ask her all my questions another time.

There's an old saying, 'Friends are the family you choose for yourself', and it had definitely been my friends who'd supported me during the toughest times in my adult life. But I couldn't help being intrigued by Daisy; she was warm, emotional and her letters were very loving towards me. I didn't feel love for her, not yet, but maybe I would over time.

18

Meeting the Bartons

When John got home that evening I read him the 'documents' from Daisy, and once I'd finished he remarked, 'I'll say one thing for her: it seems she's a survivor, just like you.'

It was true: she'd been separated from one daughter by the occupation of Jersey, then her husband left her and she'd been forced to give another daughter away; her second husband, the love of her life, died suddenly and tragically; and finally, she'd married a third husband with whom she had four children. She must be an extraordinarily strong woman to have come through it all even remotely sane.

'And her son Pete was a good lad, I thought. It's a reflection of her parenting skills that she's brought up such a friendly individual.'

I agreed, especially when I received a letter from Pete Junior enclosing copies of all the photos he'd taken in the pub: '*We should have picked a better background – the wall-paper is falling off behind us. Still, that's not important, is it? What really counts is that we met after all these years. I only wish it was sooner because I've missed so much of your life.*' He wrote that he would pop in to visit us if his driving jobs ever brought him down south and I replied, offering him an open invitation.

Looking through the photos, the resemblance between Daisy and me was even stronger than I had noticed in the flesh: our smiles were exactly the same. Pete commented on it in his letter, so it wasn't just me imagining things. We'd already made plans for John and me to go up and stay with them at Easter, and Pete wrote that he couldn't wait to introduce us to everyone else.

Before then, in February 1987, Daisy was facing a gruelling round of medical tests. She sent me lots of documents and newspaper stories about Opren, so that I could understand what she was going through, and then, very touchingly, she wrote that she was going to name John and me as beneficiaries in her will, so that I would get a share of the payout from the drugs company after her death. She advised me that I should make a will and put John's name in it so that Eric could not claim any of the money. I wrote back that I didn't want any of her money and I thought she should spend it all on herself. She deserved it after all she had been through.

All in all, it sounded as though the legal battles were at the centre of her life, and I hoped she wasn't going to be disappointed. She really felt her 'youth' had been stolen from her by Opren.

The Opren side effects weren't Daisy's only health problems. She had an arthritic hip, which made her limp, and she had glaucoma affecting her vision; she often wrote that she had to stop writing because her hand was hurting, or her eyes were giving out. I knew about the pain of arthritis because my stepmother, Billie, was crippled by it, and I wrote back sympathising. None of Daisy's ailments were life-threatening, but they made it difficult for her to get around and lead an independent life, and that must be very hard for a strong, independent woman like her.

As the Easter meeting came closer, I asked Daisy if I could bring Graham along – who was dying to be introduced. She replied that she couldn't face meeting her new grandchildren yet. She didn't want them to see her looking so poorly. Graham was very disappointed, but we decided that there was no point in trying to change her mind. John and I would have to go on our own this time. I asked Daisy if there was a local Travelodge we should book into because I knew she lived in a one-bedroom flat, but she insisted we could stay with her.

'Oh God, I hope it's not an inflatable airbed on the sitting-room floor,' I groaned to John. But in fact, as things turned out, we had to cancel that Easter trip after I found out I was pregnant.

I'd always known I was pregnant long before I missed a period because I got a funny taste in my mouth and everything smelled different. I did a test at the doctor's and it came back positive. John was over the moon when I told him. It would have been wonderful to have a child together, albeit daunting to go back to night after night of broken sleep and the whole merry cycle of child-rearing when I was forty-four years old. (Not that I felt forty-four; I was still very fit and assumed I'd have no more trouble with child-rearing than I'd had at twenty-one.) I asked Daisy if we could postpone our meeting until I'd got through the early months of pregnancy, and she was delighted to hear she was going to be a grandmother again.

Sadly, it wasn't to be: in May 1987 I foolishly lifted a burger van onto a towing hitch and it brought on a miscarriage. It turned out I'd been carrying twins. John and I were both very upset about it – he'd always wanted twins, he said – but you just grit your teeth and carry on.

That was a difficult year in many ways, as John and I tried to provide a stable home for his daughters, but we rescheduled our trip to Leeds for mid-August. When we arrived and found our way to Daisy's retirement bungalow in Bramley, she greeted us warmly and explained that she was letting us stay in the bungalow while she slept at her daughter Mid's house. It was only a tiny one-bed place, but I was amazed by her generous hospitality, especially considering she had only known us for such a short time. There was a little front garden with a row of tall sunflowers; inside, the sitting room had a tapestry-pattern settee with wooden arms, and photos of her grandchildren covered the mantelpiece. She seemed very proud of her grandchildren, talking us through each of the pictures, describing their likes, dislikes and personalities. All in all, her home was quite bare, but it was clean and tidy.

'I made you a beef casserole,' Daisy said. 'It's in the oven so you can eat when you feel hungry.'

'Aren't you going to eat with us?' I asked, surprised.

'No, I've got to get round to Mid's. I'll be back in the morning – not too early so as to give you a chance for a lie-in. You probably never get a lie-in back home with all your work and the kids to look after.'

'We're early risers so come whenever you like.' I wanted to make the most of the weekend by seeing as much of her as I could.

Daisy hurried off but she was back at ten the next morning to show us the way to Pete Junior's house. He and his wife Anne wanted to introduce us to their two sons. They were a lovely family, and over cups of tea Pete Junior entertained us with stories of his life in the cab of his HGV. Daisy didn't talk much but watched over us all with a benign smile, seeming pleased to see the two parts of her family brought together at last. I'd wondered in a corner of my brain whether she might invite Sheila along, but there was no mention of her and I assumed she must live too far away. It was strange that no one talked about her. I couldn't figure it out at all, but I supposed the story would emerge in due course.

We left Pete Junior's after a couple of hours and stopped for lunch in a pub, at last getting a chance to talk to Daisy on her own. John bought her a glass of wine and we all ordered our food. While we waited for it to arrive I began to chat.

'I think I told you that I've been in touch with Henri Le Gresley Noël's wife and daughter. I wondered if you wanted to hear about them or see photos?'

She snorted. 'Why would I want to know anything about him?'

'You must have been married to him for quite a while. Sheila was born before you left Jersey and I wasn't born till 1943. But I suppose it was hard when he volunteered for the army. Did you see much of him after that?'

'Hardly at all. Only when they were on leave.'

'Well, you must have seen him in the summer of 1942,' I teased. 'That must be when I was conceived. Where were you staying then?'

She frowned. 'I can't remember. We never had a home together. I was mostly staying with my sister Joyce.'

'In High Wycombe?'

'Yeah.' She drained her glass. 'You couldn't get me another drink, could you, love?'

John went to the bar to get her a refill and Daisy grabbed my arm. 'Look, I understand you wanting to discover the past, I really do. It's just that some periods are too painful to go back to. The past is the past, history is history. I expect you understand what I mean by that. You don't want to sit around talking about Eric all afternoon, do you?'

'No … But it would be nice to know what my father was like,' I said wistfully.

'He was handsome …'

'Yes, I've seen some photos.'

'… and he was a rotter who ran off with a Welshwoman.' She shrugged. 'Men! Who would have 'em? Except you've got a good 'un there. Take it from me.'

She pointed across to where John had engaged the barman in a lively conversation. He was the extrovert of the two of us and I tended to shelter in his shadow in company. Everyone liked John. It was impossible not to.

'Daisy, do you think it would be possible for me to meet Sheila? I'd just really like to say hello. I'm curious to see what she's like.'

Daisy pursed her lips and thought about this. 'Hmm. I'm not entirely sure what she's up to just now, but I'll see …'

'Which area does she live in?'

'Somewhere near Southampton when I last heard from her. I'll check and let you know.'

It was clear she didn't want to talk about Sheila, and pinning her down on why was like getting blood from a stone. I'd just have to keep nudging her until she consented to introduce us. It felt like the final missing link in the family chain. Sheila was older than me and she would surely be able to answer some of the questions that Daisy couldn't. And she was my full sister, unlike the Barton girls, so I hoped we would be alike, both physically and in our personalities.

After our lunch, we all got back into the car and drove to Lizzie's house, where we met her and her two girls. She and I immediately discovered that we were both horsey, and we talked at length about our horses. Afternoon tea was served and Mid dropped in to say hello, so the only one of Daisy's children I hadn't met was Sally. She was tied up that weekend and sent her apologies. It was lovely chatting with the girls, who were both open, friendly women.

We stayed a couple of hours then drove back to Daisy's home. She showed us a restaurant where we could eat that evening but declined our invitation to join us, saying she needed to rest after all the rushing around.

'We'll have to leave early in the morning,' I said. 'About ten? We have to get back for the girls.'

'Don't worry,' Daisy replied. 'I'll be round by half nine to say cheerio and get the keys from you.'

She arrived the next morning as we were busy loading up the car. There were warm hugs and promises to meet up again before too long, and all too soon the visit was over.

As John and I drove back down the motorway towards Kent, he asked, 'So? What do you think of your new family, then?'

'They're all nice,' I said. 'They couldn't have made us feel more welcome. But they don't really feel like my family. They're a self-contained unit, with childhood memories and experiences in common, and I'm just a stranger glancing off the surface of their lives. Finding my family is tougher than I expected.'

19

A Wedding and
a Funeral

Daisy didn't come down to see us in Maidstone but Pete Junior turned up one night and parked his gigantic truck outside our house, causing lots of curtain-twitching by the neighbours.

'I had a drop in Kent and thought it would be nice to see my big sis,' he said, grinning.

Unfortunately, Graham and Helen weren't at home, but he met my stepdaughters Sam and Emma and we all had a lovely evening. John told him about his market stalls and burger vans and Pete chatted about where he went in his lorry, and described to us the difficulties of getting through the Pennines in winter when the twisty mountain roads were covered in black ice or deep snow.

Helen was back from Turkey now, and I kept trying to arrange a way for her and Graham to meet their grandmother – perhaps around Christmas 1987 – but Daisy's

143

health woes were getting worse. She wrote that her solicitor was trying to negotiate an interim payment with the Opren manufacturers so that she could go into a private nursing home and have her eyes seen to. She wrote to tell me that she was so sorry not to be meeting her grandchildren, but that she wouldn't want them, or any other of the grandchildren, to see her as she was at the moment. I wrote back that Helen and Graham were disappointed but we all understood, and instead we just exchanged Christmas cards by post.

One day in January 1988, John asked me if I would come through to Canterbury with him. I tended not to go there any more, since leaving Eric and giving up my chiropody clients, but I assumed John must have had business to attend to so I went along. Once there he said, 'Can we go and have a look round the cathedral? I've never been inside.' So we went in, making our way through the hordes of tourists you find there no matter when you drop in. He stopped when we were standing right beneath the Bell Harry Tower, looking up at the amazing fan vaults hundreds of feet above us.

'I want you always to remember this moment,' John said. He took both my hands in his and asked, 'Will you marry me?'

It was the last thing I'd been expecting, and all I could do was stutter out, 'Yes.' We'd both known since the early days of the relationship that we wanted to spend our lives together, but there didn't seem any rush to marry, especially after the trauma of getting through our respective divorces. When he asked me, though, I was moved beyond measure and there was no question that I would accept. It was an incredibly romantic proposal.

A couple of weeks later, John took me out for dinner in a quiet Italian restaurant we both liked and presented me with a lovely diamond solitaire ring. I thought, 'How nice that it's just low-key and personal, between the two of us!' Then when we got back to the house, there was a huge shriek of 'Surprise!' and all our friends leapt out into the hallway. John had only gone and organised an engagement party, complete with buffet and bar, without telling me. He was a bit of a devil for surprise parties!

Although we didn't have much money at the time, we planned to have a good old knees-up of a wedding at which all our extended family members could meet each other. We picked a date in September to give everyone plenty of time to book a couple of days off work and make travel arrangements. I hoped all my new siblings could be there, and most of all I wanted Daisy to make it.

In response to my invitation Daisy wrote a very emotional letter: '*What a wonderful caring, loving daughter you are.*' She apologised that she would not be able to pay for our wedding – which I hadn't for one moment expected her to do – and said, '*No mother could wish for a better man than John for you. I love him!*'

Her health problems continued, though. She was in a lot of pain and taking morphine. Sometimes she took herself off to a Roman Catholic retreat to stay for a week or two in solitude in a chalet in their grounds. '*It's lovely and peaceful,*' she wrote, '*sort of stepping off the world for a while. No religion or anything like that. Only peace.*'

Maybe I should have been alarmed by news of her ongoing health worries, but whenever I had seen her she had appeared as fit as a fiddle, so I didn't give it as much thought as I should have. As the wedding date approached, I was tied up with all the myriad arrangements and wasn't in touch with Daisy as frequently as I had been the previous year, but I was delighted to hear that her Opren lawsuit was finally settled. She got far less than the millions she'd been expecting, but enough to buy a nice chalet-style mobile home by the sea. She invited us to visit, saying, 'You must come some day,' but didn't name a date because it depended on her health.

We didn't have the time that summer. Daisy wrote in one letter that she might not be able to come to the wedding because of her health, but then in the next said she would definitely be there: 'I will be coming to your wedding, so help me.' As the date drew near she sent a wedding present of a cut-glass bell, which was very pretty.

Our big day, 17 September 1988, dawned and I got dressed in a pale pink suit with the oversized eighties shoulder pads and a matching hat. I'd bought some beautiful cream shoes with a pink leather stripe, but there was a problem: nine weeks before the wedding my horse stood on my foot, breaking the big toe and slicing off the nail. I was determined not to let those shoes go to waste, but I had to down a large brandy and some paracetamol in order to force my poor foot into that shoe.

The ceremony was in Maidstone Methodist Church. I'd wanted a proper church service, since I didn't have one first time around, and it was a beautiful white-painted building with arched windows and pointy turrets. I hobbled down the aisle in my agonising shoe, then when I got to the front I turned and scanned the rows of guests, looking for Daisy. I hoped that Graham would have guided her and the other Bartons down to sit in the family pews at the front, but there was no sign of them. Could the traffic have been bad? Maybe they were stuck in a queue in the Dartford Tunnel and would sneak in at the back when they arrived.

John and I made our vows and were pronounced 'man and wife', and it was very emotional and moving. All the words of the ceremony made total sense to me because at last I was with the man I wanted to grow old with, the man I wanted to look after in sickness and health. As we walked out of the church to have our group photos taken, I couldn't see Daisy anywhere. Graham and Helen had been looking forward to meeting her and I'd been desperate to have my one remaining 'parent' there, but I got on with what was otherwise a perfect day.

Needless to say, as soon as we got into the car outside the church I took my shoes off and breathed a sigh of pure relief. We held our knees-up at the Mote Park Pavilion in Maidstone, with a buffet, bar and disco, and the festivities went on till the wee small hours. I danced barefoot, of course; those gorgeous shoes never got worn again. Afterwards, we stayed in a luxurious caravan owned by John's sister and her husband, then we jumped in our van the next morning to find that some friends had stuffed confetti into the air conditioning and tied tin cans on the back, all in traditional style. Our honeymoon was an idyllic week in Majorca, just the two of us. It couldn't have been more perfect.

On our return I telephoned Daisy to see what had happened to her.

'Oh, I'm so sorry, my darling. I can't apologise enough. I'd bought a new mother-of-the-bride dress and I was standing in the hall, all ready to come, just waiting for Pete, when I collapsed. It was a really bad turn. Pete had to carry me through to the sofa and call a doctor, and all the time I was crying, "I have to go to Cherry's wedding, please let me go!" I'll never forgive myself for missing it.'

'Never mind. Are you all right now?'

'As much as I can be,' she said. 'Now, tell me all about your big day. I can't wait to see the photographs!'

I described the wedding and honeymoon, but we agreed it would be easiest to show the photographs to her in person, so we arranged to meet soon afterwards at a spot halfway between us, a pub Pete Senior recommended that was just off a dual carriageway.

When the day came John and I drove up there, taking our wedding photo album, and found a table inside. The meeting time came and went, and we waited and waited, until eventually Pete Senior turned up on his own.

'I'm afraid she didn't feel up to coming,' he said as he walked in.

My face flushed. 'What do you mean? Why not?'

'She's having a bit of a panic attack,' he explained. 'Same thing as happened before your wedding.'

'Come on, let me buy you a drink,' John said.

We had a drink with Pete then turned and headed for home. On the telephone the next day Daisy was apologetic and wanted to set up another meeting, but it never happened. In fact, I never saw Daisy again. One morning I got a telephone call from Mid, who was sobbing as she tried to get her words out. Straight away, I guessed.

'Is it Daisy?'

'She died last night. In her sleep. Dad was beside her.'

I got goosebumps all over and sat down hard on a chair. I hadn't known Daisy well enough for her death to be a huge personal tragedy, but I was shocked that she had gone, just like that. I'd assumed Daisy and I still had years to become close. She was too young to die. I bitterly regretted that I hadn't made more effort to go up to Leeds, spend time with her and try to dig out all the fragments of the past she held in her memory. I still felt I hadn't bonded with her very well, although we had corresponded and phoned each other regularly. The woman I had known was loving and friendly, and I knew I was going to miss her.

'I'm so sorry for your loss,' I told Mid. 'Let me know if there's anything I can do. And be sure to tell me when the funeral is because I'll definitely come up for it.'

First, there had to be an autopsy to establish the cause of death, because Daisy had died at home rather than in a hospital. A funeral date was set, and on that morning we had already set off to drive north in Graham's car when Mid called me on our big old mobile phone – it was like a brick with a handle, state of the art back then – to tell me the funeral had to be postponed because they were holding a second autopsy. When the delayed funeral date finally came around, John and I and Graham and his wife

Fiona drove up to Mid's house so we could follow the family cars to a Leeds crematorium. It was every bit as grim as these places usually are, with a big brick chimney pointing up into overcast grey skies. Pete Junior had told me that Daisy never liked wreaths, so I took a spray bouquet instead.

It was a simple service, very short. I couldn't hold back the tears and Pete Senior passed me his handkerchief while John kept his arm tightly around me. Afterwards, I assumed there would be some kind of wake, a gathering at which we shared memories of Daisy over tea and cake, but Pete Senior said they were all just heading home. I looked round the mourners and asked the million-dollar question: 'Where's Sheila? Which one is she?'

'We didn't know how to get in touch with her,' Mid replied, 'so I don't think she knows Mum has died.'

On a day that was strange for me anyway as I mourned the mother I'd only just been beginning to get to know, whom I'd only met twice, that seemed the saddest thing of all.

20

Looking for Sheila

I've always been the kind of person who can move on from sad experiences. I don't dwell on them: I live them, sort them, then get on with the rest of my life. But it was hard to move on after Daisy's death because there were so many loose ends and unanswered questions. At the risk of stating the obvious, death is final. There's no going back to ask questions you forgot to ask, or to say what you meant to say but never got round to. Lots of Daisy's secrets had gone to the crematorium with her, and there were things I had to accept I would never know now.

I was also sad that Graham and Helen never met her. Looking back, for all the love she expressed for me in her letters, Daisy never really became part of my life. She never visited my home, she never met my children, she didn't come to my wedding. I went through a stage of feeling quite angry about that. But, then, they say that anger is one of the stages of grief, something you just have to get through and come out the other side.

The rest of my life was wonderful. In the first years of our marriage John and I just got closer and closer every day. We began spending weekends away, visiting key places from each other's past: we went to Canvey Island, where John was reunited with a half-sister and a half-brother whom he hadn't seen for ages; we travelled to Wiltshire so I could show him Glebe House in West Lavington and some other sites from my childhood; and we decided to fly out to Jersey for a weekend, just to wander around and familiarise ourselves with the island. It was wintertime and bitterly cold, but we wrapped up in lots of layers and braved the chill winds. Most hotels and guesthouses were closed for the season, but we found one near the waterfront with a very accommodating landlady who gave us an extra thick quilt to stick on top of the big double bed.

Our weekend was spent walking the streets and ducking into cafés, restaurants or pubs when we were hungry or when the cold started to gnaw at our bones. Food was very important to John ... he was a big man with a large appetite! At the landlady's recommendation, we taxied over to a seafood restaurant called Pedro's on the other side of the St Helier bay, and there we dined on luxurious, lip-smacking platters of lobster and Jersey Royals.

One day, while we were wandering around the town, we found ourselves in the square outside the Renoufs' flat. I pointed out to John the home of the distant cousins I'd visited with Eric and he asked, 'Do you want to go in and say hello? They might be able to help you find Sheila.'

I thought about it for a moment but decided I wasn't ready. I still felt bruised by the experience of getting to know Daisy and then losing her again, and didn't want to set myself up for more rejection. Besides, I felt very loved by John and my children so there was no urgent need to find any other family members.

'Let's just leave it,' I decided. 'I can write to them from home.' I scribbled down their address, which had got mislaid when I left Canterbury. We took some photos in the square outside, John holding the camera at arm's length to fit both of us in the shot. Lots of photographs were taken that weekend, and we look blissfully happy and relaxed in all of them.

Later that evening, back at the guesthouse, we got chatting to our landlady and I told her about the search for my missing sister.

'Whereabouts did the family live?' she asked. 'I might know someone who knows them.'

'Bellozanne Valley,' I told her. 'Is that anywhere near here?'

She scratched her head, looking puzzled. 'I've lived in Jersey all my life and I've never heard of it.'

That was odd. I supposed it must have changed its name over the years. 'My father was born in Ville à l'Evêque. Do you know that?'

'Oh sure, that's farming country in the northeast of the island. You won't find much up there except Jersey cows.'

'My father's job when he lived here was farm labourer.'

'Yes, that's the only work available in that part of the island.'

I tried to think of other local information she might be able to help us with. 'I wonder which hospital Sheila would have been born in. Maybe they would keep records of births back before the war. Trouble is, I don't know her exact date of birth. Only that it was before the war.'

'There was a new hospital built in 1938. The old maternity hospital was closed around that time. Perhaps they transferred the records across but I somehow doubt it. I'll ask around for you, mind. Sheila Noël, you said the name was?'

'She may have changed her name if she's married, but I think that's what she was christened.'

'I'll ask around and let you know if I find anything.'

The landlady was St Helier born and bred, and told us she would rather live there than anywhere else in the world. She loved the land, the sea, the people, the peace and the beauty of the place.

'Don't you ever get bored?' John asked. He was a people person and thrived on a full social calendar and something different to do every night of the week. I'd never known anyone who had quite so many friends.

'It's far too busy for me in summer,' she said. 'I look forward to a bit of peace and tranquillity in the winter months when the tourists have gone home. I prefer it then.'

I knew what she meant. Despite the cold weather and rough, grey seas, I found the quietness of the place very healing. It was unspoiled and natural, with a real island feel and a culture all its own.

Our weekend there was completely different from my previous visit with Eric because I was with a man I loved, who knew instinctively when I needed a cuddle, when I wanted to talk and when I preferred silence and the space to process my thoughts. I didn't cry on the journey back this time, but my thoughts turned once again to Sheila, the sister I'd never met. Maybe I would have one more go at finding her.

Daisy had once mentioned that Sheila had a French middle name – Marguerite – and I decided to place an advert in the *Jersey Evening News* in the hope that her name would be unusual enough for someone to recognise it. My advert read: *'I'm trying to trace Sheila*

Marguerite Noël, who was born in Jersey just before the war. I believe I am her sister. If you have any information, please contact me.' I gave a PO Box number and crossed my fingers.

'What makes you think she is on the island?' John asked. 'I thought Daisy said she was in the Southampton area.'

'You never know. Maybe a family member will spot the advert and contact her.' I'd paid for it to run for a fortnight.

I decided to run it in the *Southampton Daily Echo* as well, in case she was still there. It was a long shot, but maybe someone would recognise the name Sheila Marguerite Noël, even if she had married and taken a new surname.

And finally I wrote to the Renoufs, telling them about Daisy's death, in case they hadn't heard via any other route. No Jersey relatives had turned up at the funeral, so perhaps her brother Bernard and sister Joyce didn't know. I told them that I had met Daisy twice and had been in correspondence with her, but that she hadn't got round to introducing me to Sheila and I was very keen to get in touch if anyone there had an address for her.

It would be lovely to find this woman who was my only living full blood relative. Although I very much liked all the Barton children, I felt we would only be on Christmas card terms as the years went by. I had my own family with John and the children, but thoughts of my missing sister nagged at me. It was tantalising to know that Sheila was out there somewhere, leading her own life, possibly raising her own children – my nephews and nieces – but with no knowledge of my existence. If only I could find her, I was sure it would enrich both of our lives. Siblings have a special kind of closeness, a relaxed trust in each other that it would be lovely to experience. I knew if anything bad ever happened to Graham, Helen would be there in a flash, and vice versa, even though they both had their own lives. *If only I could find Sheila. If only.*

A letter came back from Phyllis Renouf, thanking me for letting them know about Daisy and saying that they were sorry but they couldn't help with the search for Sheila, because none of the relatives seemed to have any idea where she was. She said she would write again if Sheila got in touch but she had no other suggestions. That was a blow.

Still, I hoped maybe there would be a reply to one of my adverts looking for Sheila, but nothing at all came back. I racked my brains, trying to think of other ways I could try to trace her, and then life took over and I became immersed in new problems of a more pressing nature when the meat plant where John and I worked closed down.

It was hard for John to get another job because he wasn't able to read or write, but he started helping a friend on his burger van while I managed to get a short-term contract working in the sauna at a swimming pool complex in Maidstone. I greeted customers, sold tickets, handed out the towels and told people where to go, then provided soft drinks in the relaxation area. It was good fun but unfortunately didn't pay enough to keep us all. The bills were pouring in, and it was an anxious time.

The swimming pool complex was about to close for refurbishment when, one day, I heard overheard the chap in charge of the refurb saying that he needed to find caterers for the three hundred builders on their site, and I had one of my rare brainwaves.

'Excuse me,' I interrupted. 'My husband could do that. He runs a burger van at the moment but he has *lots* of catering experience.'

It was a bit of an exaggeration but I knew John was a good cook, who'd started way back as a teenager when he learned to make pies for his dad's butcher's shop. He'd always had the gift of blagging, and when he went for a meeting with the building site manager he walked away with the contract. Soon, he and I were catering for three building sites, a racetrack and the men working on a new hotel under construction. The work was full on, 24/7. I'd get up at 4 a.m. to collect the rolls for the day from a bakery then drive a 72-mile round trip dropping off supplies and clean linen at the various sites. There was tea and toast served at 7 a.m., a full English breakfast around 8 to 9, a huge lunch at 12 – maybe cottage pie, lasagne, burgers and chips, apple pie and custard – then on some sites we did an evening meal at 5, as well as catering for site meetings and parties. After that, I'd take the dirty linen home and get the washing machine running, and it was up to do the whole routine again at 4 the following morning. It was exhausting and constantly challenging, but John and I much preferred being our own bosses to taking orders from other people, and the money was better than we could have earned in any one job.

I was working in a site canteen one day in 1991 when Helen phoned with the wonderful news that she was pregnant. I announced it to the room and all these burly workmen gave a huge cheer. Nine months later I was with Helen from within minutes of receiving the middle-of-the-night phone call, right the way through a tricky labour, and my heart just swelled with love when I held that little mite in my arms for the first time. It was miraculous becoming a grandmother to that little girl they named Hannah. I know everyone says it, but she genuinely was the most beautiful creature I'd ever seen, with her tiny little fingers and bright, curious eyes! It was quite a different feeling from holding Helen for the first time because now I could enjoy this child who carried my DNA without responsibility. She came as a special gift, an extension of my family through no effort of my own.

A few months after Hannah's birth, John and I decided that we were fed up with working all the hours God gave. You can do that for a while, but life is short and you have to have time to enjoy yourself as well as earning money or it's simply not worth it. We had fallen in love with the North Devon countryside after John started going clay-shooting there with a group of friends, and we began the process of selling our businesses in Kent so we could relocate. Sam and Emma stayed in the Maidstone house with their boyfriends while John and I trundled down the M4 with a horsebox (at that time I had a pony called Cindylou and a horse called Kali), three dogs and a few ferrets.

We started off living in a caravan overlooking Lee Bay, near Woolacombe, where I set up a little pony trekking business with just a field, a barn and a few borrowed horses. There was no water or electricity, but the view over the Bristol Channel was knockout. In spring and summer the hedgerows were resplendent with bright red wildflowers causing locals to call the area 'Fuchsia Valley'. I had time to get out and ride my horses through the woods and across the hills instead of just dashing by to check up on them twice a day, as I'd been doing in Kent. While I managed the ponies, John set up a new market stall down there, and we breathed a sigh of relief, planning to take life a lot easier as we approached our sixtieth birthdays.

And just when it looked as though our lives were getting a little calmer and more settled, I had a phone call to say that Billie, my stepmother, was being admitted to a hospice up in Scarborough. She'd taken herself off to private nursing homes in the past and had usually been asked to leave after falling out with other residents or just generally being obnoxious. But when I rang and spoke to the manager of this particular hospice, she told me that Billie didn't have long to live. And despite our history, I knew I had to go up and see her.

21

Making Peace
with Billie

Since Pop died, Billie had been living in the same house in Scarborough, propped up by visits from carers, who did her shopping, cooking and cleaning. By the early 1990s she was bedridden and needed the carers to bath and change her as well. I worried about her but was too far away to do anything practical to help. I phoned frequently and kept her up to date with the family news, but it's a long way from Devon to Scarborough, so it was quite a while since I'd actually seen her.

I got a shock when I arrived at the hospice. Billie had always been a tall, commanding presence, but now she had become shrunk and twisted with the ravages of arthritis. Her hands were gnarled, knotted and as stiff as wood. Her shoulders were hunched, head scrunched down to her chest in a way that looked horribly uncomfortable. The pain must have been horrendous.

She was strong, though. She had outlived Pop by a decade, despite the fact that she'd had a bad heart as a child and her mother had had to push her around in a pushchair so she didn't strain it. Now that same heart was giving out, but in her eighties rather than her youth, and I sensed that she was mentally ready to go. Her only other relatives were a sister who was too elderly and frail to help, and a niece.

I always remembered something that Mum said to me when I was a young girl: 'It's nice to have someone hold your hand when you go through the door. They can't go through with you but they can be there right up till you go through.' I imagine the words stayed in my head because it's not the kind of thing you normally tell a youngster. I can't remember what age I was, but perhaps it was when Mum was ill herself, and musing out loud about the end of her own life. At any rate, I decided I would stay and see Billie up to 'the door', since there was no one else to do it.

There was a big armchair in her room at the hospice and I settled in to keep her company. Most of the time she slept, under the influence of intravenous morphine, but when she woke up we chatted about this and that. She couldn't stay awake for long, sometimes nodding off mid-sentence, which made for odd, disjointed conversation.

'My granddaughter Hannah is two now,' I told her. 'She's toddling around, all curious about the world and a complete danger to herself.'

'Who's that, then?'

'Helen's daughter. You remember Helen.'

'Oh, yes.' There was a long silence and I couldn't tell if she was awake or asleep, so I waited.

'Your dad and I never understood why you married that Eric,' Billie said out of the blue. 'I think you're well out of that one.'

'Really? Pop never tried to talk me out of marrying him at the time,' I replied.

'There was never any point trying to talk you out of anything. You made up your own mind and that was that.'

I thought that wasn't strictly true – she'd stopped me from studying agriculture for starters – but I wasn't about to resurrect old arguments. Instead I told her about the life John and I had made for ourselves in Devon, and how much I enjoyed running the trekking stables.

'That's one thing we always had in common,' Billie said. 'You and I were both animal lovers.'

I remembered her giving away our goat, Grizelda, and bit my tongue. 'I love horses. My son Graham has got the bug as well.'

'Your John, though,' she whispered. 'He's a good man.' We'd been up to visit her a couple of times and John had fixed a few things round the house for her and charmed her with his cheery conversation.

'I'm glad you like him,' I said. 'He sends you his best, by the way.'

Billie had fallen asleep, though, so I took out my book, thankful I'd remembered to bring one. I whiled away the day chatting to the staff, reading or slipping out to phone John and check everything was all right down south. When night came I slept in the chair in Billie's room. Deaths from heart failure are often in the early hours of the morning, so I drifted in and out of sleep listening to her weak, raspy breathing, alert for any changes that would signal the end. Morning came, and she was still with us, then another day passed, but every day the periods when she was awake got fewer and further between.

'How long do you think you'll be?' John asked on the phone. I had no way of knowing the answer, but the hospice staff seemed to think death was imminent so there was no way I could just leave.

More days went by, and then a week, and still Billie hung on. Her heart may have been weak when she was little, but the nurses were amazed by its resilience now. She clung to life with grim determination, heartbeat after heartbeat.

'I did love you, you know,' she said one day, resting her gnarled old hand on mine, but her eyes were closed and I wasn't sure she knew it was me.

'Thank you,' I replied. I couldn't lie by saying I'd loved her back, but it was nice that we had made our peace. She couldn't help the way she had treated me; we are all a product of our upbringings and she did what she thought was best in the circumstances. Besides, I'd now experienced the tricky path you tread as a stepmother – you're not a 'real' parent, but you need to be able to exert authority sometimes and that can cause resentment. I could sympathise with Billie over that, at least.

After I'd been with her for two weeks, spending every night in the chair in her room and every day, at her bedside, Billie finally passed away very peacefully. She hadn't been conscious at all during that last day, and her breathing just got fainter and fainter then stopped. I'd witnessed several deaths when I worked in hospitals in Kent, and one time an old chap had died during a chiropody appointment with me, so I knew what the physical process was like, but I found Billie's passing very spiritual and moving. I wasn't sad about it; she had reached a decent age and had led a pretty full life. We had never been close, but it felt like the closing of another door to my past. She was one more person whom I would never be able to question again. It was the end of a particular era.

I stayed up in Scarborough to arrange Billie's funeral: a simple Jehovah's Witness funeral service at the crematorium and then a wake back at Billie's house with the few friends she had left. One of them came up to me during the wake and said, 'You do realise, don't you, dear, that Billie had left the Jehovah's Witnesses? She changed her mind about all that, went right off them.'

'Did she?' Oops-a-daisy! I'd thought I was doing the right thing by her, but it seemed I'd made the ultimate *faux pas* in giving her the wrong kind of funeral. No matter; frankly, I didn't believe it would make the remotest difference to the destination of her soul.

22

Going Bust and Climbing Back Up Again

John and I had moved out of the caravan and were renting an old farmhouse in Devon, but when Billie's estate was settled I inherited enough money to put a deposit on Gabriel's Meadow Cottage in North Molton, a traditional little cottage with a tiny garden and a barn. It had an odd design. There were two parts, with a bedroom and large bathroom above the main room, then some steps down to the other side where a winding staircase led up to a second bedroom with a sloping beamed roof. The only disadvantage was that if you slept in the second bedroom, you had a long trek if you happened to need the loo in the middle of the night!

We both loved Devon and never had any regrets about leaving Kent. My horses were in a field just down the road from our house and there was plenty of beautiful countryside to ride them in. John could go out and do his clay-pigeon shooting, and he bought a gun shop in Barnstaple, which he loved running. The children were all doing well and we thought we had it made. And it's just at moments like that when life decides to throw you a curveball …

First of all, I had to give up the trekking business after being unable to agree ongoing terms with the guy who loaned the horses to me. Then the BSE crisis and the tightening of shotgun licensing laws meant that farmers were buying fewer guns. And finally, after the horrific massacre at Dunblane in March 1996, when Thomas Hamilton killed sixteen schoolchildren and one teacher, new acts were passed in Parliament which made private ownership of handguns illegal. What had been a thriving gun shop went bust in the space of six months, and John had no option but to declare bankruptcy. To make matters worse, I'd put his name on the title deeds of the cottage, and on Christmas Eve 1996 I got a phone call from the solicitors handling the bankruptcy to say that they were going to repossess it and we were being made homeless. I screamed down the phone, 'I hope when you sit down to your Christmas dinner with your family, you choke on your turkey!' I became so hysterical that John had to wrest the receiver away from me. It completely ruined Christmas for us that year, but once I'd calmed down I managed to negotiate a deal whereby I sold the cottage myself within six weeks and gave the creditors the money they were owed, keeping anything left over myself. I figured I'd get a better deal than some bankruptcy solicitors, and so it proved when I walked away with the princely sum of five grand to my name.

It took us a long time to climb back up from bankruptcy, and we did it by working flat out. Fortunately, we were both hard grafters. John went back to Kent to spend three days a week running stalls in three different markets, and he got a job harvesting withies (willow wands) on a farm near us in Devon. I worked four nights on, four nights off in a meat factory, and on my nights off I worked in an old people's home. We managed to get a pitch for a burger van in South Molton and ran that as well.

It was a tough period. I was constantly tired, and for the first time in my life I succumbed to depression. What was the point of working so hard when everything could be taken away from you in the snap of your fingers, through no fault of your own? I'd thought John and I were blessed, that we were lucky, but the bankruptcy was a spectacular piece of bad luck.

'Come on, love,' John said. 'We're through the worst now. We're strong people. We'll find a way to get back to where we were in no time.'

I couldn't seem to pick myself up, though. When the alarm went off in the morning I just wanted to pull the covers over my head. Nothing could cheer me up – not even visits from my lovely grandchildren. (By this time Graham and his wife Fiona had two children, Jacob and Meghan, and lived in London, while Helen had Hannah, a bright little spark who was thriving at primary school.) I lost my appetite and had to force myself to eat, and I wasn't sleeping very well even though I was dog tired, which made things worse. I couldn't be bothered to look after my appearance, and I was irritable with John: in short, I was suffering the classic symptoms of depression.

When I finally went to my GP about it, he told me that I was a strong person and I should pull myself together, so I struggled on for another year. Finally, in 1998, I burst into tears while talking to a locum in the practice and he referred me to a counsellor. She was a lovely woman, but I found it hard to talk to her.

'Tell me about your parents,' she asked at the first session, and I quipped, 'How long have you got?'

At her urging, I ran through the bare bones of my story: adopted, Mum dies, difficult relationship with stepmother, trace birth father to find he's already passed away, difficult first marriage, Pop dies, look for birth mother and find her but she dies before telling me what I want to know, then stepmother dies and my second husband goes bankrupt and I lose my home.

'Wow!' she said. 'No wonder you're depressed. You have dozens of reasons right there.' She began to go through my story bit by bit, asking detailed questions like, 'How did that make you feel?' and, 'Did you feel rejected by so-and-so?'

I answered her in as few words as possible: 'Not too bad', 'Not really'.

She tried to dig deeper: 'You were your mum and dad's number one before the age of nine, but after your mum's death there was always someone else who seemed to come first. Perhaps you came to believe that you didn't deserve to be happy. Perhaps that's why you don't seem to value yourself.'

'Maybe.'

'I suspect that's why you've often failed to stand up for yourself. You could have demanded that Daisy answered your questions, but you say you "didn't like to impose". Actually, you had every right to impose. She owed you an explanation.'

'Hmm.'

'But you find it difficult to express your emotions simply because you've been discouraged from doing so right through your teens and your first marriage, back from the moment your dad asked you not to cry but to be a brave girl.'

'I suppose so.'

'Strong emotions, whether happy or sad, feel scary to you so you've learned, very successfully, to block them out. The problem is that they don't entirely go away. They remain beneath the surface, and over time they can fester and cause symptoms like the depression you're going through just now.'

'So what do I do about it?'

'You talk to me, and gradually we'll bring those feelings out into the open and make them feel less scary.'

That sounded a bit of a tall order, but I think the sessions we had together helped me a bit without ever 'curing' me completely. What helped more was that John and I found ourselves a new and lucrative business venture. From talking to clients at the burger van, I managed to get a contract catering for the canteen at a local engineering plant, and John came in to help me. We began doing outside catering from that big commercial kitchen and one day, in the year 2000, John was asked to go and carve at a friend's pig-roast barbecue. I went along with him, examined the spit, tasted the succulent meat it produced and said, 'I want one of those.' The very next day we went out and bought ourselves one and set up our own brand new business.

We were the first pig-roasting business in the area and trade soon took off. Sometimes we catered for as many as five weddings in a weekend; we had concessions at some big manor houses, where we did Medieval or Tudor-style banquets; and we could be hired for any corporate dinner, barbecue or family event – you name it, we did it. John tended to look after the pig while I made loads of different kinds of salads and desserts, and before long our finances were back in the black again. I had muscles like a coal heaver from carrying all our equipment around, but we had a sound business with bookings stretching almost a year ahead.

John was the sociable one when we were at work, while I hid behind him, but I could be tough when it came to business. He was the nice guy and I was the old cow who insisted on getting a cheque in advance and making sure it cleared into our account before the big day, thank you very much. We weren't going to get stung, not if I had anything to do with it.

Gradually, I came out of my shell. I learned how to be a sociable person just by watching the way John operated: he'd remember people's names from one occasion to the next, and ask after their spouses/children/dogs; he'd tease them a little but not too much; he'd always seem cheerful (faking it if necessary); he'd make sure everyone was part of the fun and no one was hanging round the edges feeling shy; and he was loud, so you couldn't possibly ignore him. Partly he was using the skills he'd honed as a family butcher – where he chatted up the old ladies, making risqué jokes about sausages and so forth – but mostly he genuinely cared about people and enjoyed getting to know them. A ridiculously large number of people considered him one of their closest friends. That's just how he was.

Business was in the forefront of my mind in those years – that and John, my children and grandchildren, and my horses. I was still in touch with the Bartons from time to time, but just quick 'how are you?' phone calls. My thoughts sometimes turned to Sheila, and I wondered if anyone had told her yet that Daisy had died. I was pretty sure that she didn't know of my existence. Sometimes I wondered how she was and what was happening in her life. If a letter arrived in the post with handwriting I didn't recognise, I always had a moment of excitement, wondering if it might be from or about her. I had no idea where she was living or what she looked like: she could have lived in the next village to us and I wouldn't have known. I could be passing her in the supermarket once a week without having a clue. I had more or less given up hope of getting in touch with her because I'd tried everything I could think of to no avail. But life was sweet again, so I wasn't as desperate as I had felt at tougher times.

23

Shadows Blot
Out the Sun

By June 2006, our pig-roasting business had been running for six years. John and I were sixty-three years old and beginning to think about selling the business. That summer John complained of feeling tired a lot. We had a particularly busy season, with wall-to-wall bookings, so I didn't give it a second thought. He'd just had an operation to ease the arthritis in one of his wrists and was in plaster from fingers to elbow, so that didn't help. He was upset about it because it meant he couldn't cast a fly rod, and John loved his fly fishing. Later in the summer, when he was still feeling exhausted, I persuaded him to go to the doctor, but he was basically told that it wasn't unusual for a man of his age, doing physical work, and that he should be sure to rest up over the winter, when bookings traditionally dropped off.

In January he needed a second operation on his wrist, and that meant yet more plaster (and more time away from his beloved fishing). He still felt knackered and he was getting frequent tummy upsets as well. Then, in March 2007, during a pig-roast booking, John found he couldn't lift a gas bottle. It simply wouldn't budge when he strained with all his strength. That rang alarm bells for me, because he'd always been such a big, strong giant of a man and he used to toss these bottles around without much effort. This time the doctor said he thought it might be some kind of muscular problem and sent him off for a battery of tests and scans, but they found nothing. I assumed he was just experiencing muscle loss associated with ageing; most of us who are in our sixties have bits that don't work quite as well as they used to. We carried on working, and I had to be the one who did any heavy lifting. Fortunately, I was strong as an ox so it wasn't a problem for me.

By the end of April, right at the beginning of our busy season, John felt so ill he could barely get out of bed. I remember watching him one morning, leaning on the bedside table and needing all his strength to push himself up to standing. Sometimes he would scream with pain when all he was doing was sitting in a chair, and he'd go white as a sheet as he adjusted his position, trying to ease the agony.

'This is not normal. You have to go back to the doctor and ask for a second opinion,' I told him. 'This is not just the aches and pains of ageing.' When you live and work with someone day in, day out you don't always notice when they look under the weather, but I suddenly realised that John had lost a lot of weight; he looked haggard and his skin had a sickly yellowish tinge. All of a sudden, I remembered telling Mum that she looked like a Chinaman. Could there be something wrong with his liver? Could it be jaundice? 'I'm making an appointment for you if you won't do it yourself,' I told him, and at last he let me.

The doctor took one look at him and admitted him to the Medical Assessment Unit at our local hospital for tests. For two weeks I lived on my nerves, heart in my mouth, as I struggled to keep the business going by the seat of my pants then rushed in to see John at every visiting hour. I liked the consultant, a young Indian chap, who was determined to find out what was going on. John's blood tests were giving very unusual results, and this man assured us that he wouldn't rest till he discovered why. He made it his personal mission.

Soon they were talking about biopsies and barium enemas, CAT scans and then a liver scan. I was getting a very bad feeling about it, and in the back of my mind I counted all the money we could lay our hands on if we had to get private treatment for John. I took advice on selling the business, determined that money would be no object. I wanted John to see the best people in the country. While all this was going on, as luck would have it, I got knocked out cold by one of my horses, when it went bananas and smashed me to the floor, so I was walking around with a bruised, swollen face, and later found out I'd fractured my nose and cheekbone!

'Looks as though we should admit you too?' a nurse called when I went in to visit John. 'What happened?'

'It was him,' I joked, pointing to John. Anyone looking at him would have known that wasn't true: he barely had the strength to lift a cup of tea now.

'I gave him a bed bath earlier,' the nurse told me. 'We've all been admiring his tattoos.'

John had a scene with hummingbirds and colourful hanging flowers all over his back, and koi carp on his chest. It was always a talking point when he took his shirt off.

John winked at me. 'You're not jealous about the bed baths, are you, babe?'

'Me? Naw … Saves me the trouble.'

The day came when we were called for a meeting with the consultant to hear the verdict. We sat hand in hand, and I was conscious my palm was sweaty; perhaps John's was too. He was gripping mine tightly, looking straight at the man, who was probably a couple of decades younger than us, but who held our fate in the notes and charts on his desk.

'It's not good news,' he said straight away. 'I'm afraid we've found shadows on the liver and metastases in the spine and all over the abdominal cavity.'

I felt a falling sensation, as if the ground had disappeared beneath my feet. Because of my radiography training, I knew straight away what this meant, but I wasn't sure if John did. My stomach tied itself in knots as I turned to see how he had taken it.

John looked very pale. 'So what do we do?' he asked. 'What happens next?'

'There are a few more tests we want to run then I think we'll get you in for a blood transfusion. You'll feel much stronger after that.'

'Have I had these shadows for long? Why weren't they spotted before? I first went to see the doctor last summer.'

'It's hard to say why they didn't show up in previous scans, but possibly the doctors were looking for something else at the time.'

I was struck dumb, frozen to the spot, because I knew what John hadn't realised: that it was cancer, it had spread all over the place, and this was almost certainly a death sentence. The consultant was still talking, explaining about palliative care available, and suddenly, at that word 'palliative', I burst into tears.

'Don't cry, babe,' John urged. 'I need you to be brave.'

Instantly, I was nine years old again and Pop was telling me not to cry after Mum died. *OK, I can do this*, I thought. *I'll be strong for him.* I dried my eyes and began asking the consultant practical questions about what we could do: Was it worth getting a second opinion? Why weren't they trying any drug therapy? What could we do at home to ease his symptoms? What foods should I feed him? I asked all the questions I could think of except for the one that was at the very front of my thoughts: *how long?* It was up to John whether he wanted to ask that one, and he didn't even realise that he had the Big C.

We drove home with paper bags full of medicines and my scribbled list of instructions. 'Will you call Sam and Emma?' I asked. 'Or should we invite them down for the weekend so you can tell them in person?'

'Hang on a minute, babe. I haven't even got my head round this myself,' he said.

We went back into the house as normal, picking up the post and putting the kettle on – except that it wasn't normal; it would never be normal again. John sat in his chair to look through the post and asked me about the pig-roast bookings coming up for that weekend.

'Don't worry, I'll get another chef in. You need to rest, the doctor said.'

'Yeah.' He had a faraway look in his eyes, and I knew he needed peace and quiet to process what he'd just been told. I made supper and served it just as I always did, but he could barely eat and neither could I. We watched a little telly then had an early night, and it was only when we were cuddling up in bed that John said to me, in a small, scared voice, 'I'm not going to get through this, am I?'

I hesitated, wondering if it was kinder to give him hope. 'It doesn't look good,' I said finally.

He grunted as if I'd confirmed what he'd been thinking. True acceptance of the death sentence would take longer, and he went through all the classic stages of grief: denial (maybe they'd got it wrong, surely he could beat this); anger (huge, raging anger at the doctors whom he thought had failed to spot clear symptoms the previous year); bargaining (if he took his medicines and did everything the doctor ordered, maybe he'd still have a chance); depression (horrid for me to watch and a first in our marriage – he simply never got depressed before this); and finally, an acceptance of sorts.

In news reports written after celebrities die of cancer, it always says they 'fought bravely', but I'm afraid I don't buy it. You can't *fight* cancer, for a start. You take your medicine and deal with the side effects because what else are you going to do? John was a brave, stoical man, but there were times when he was shaking in terror at the thought of dying. Neither of us was a follower of a particular religion. We both believed that spirits live on after death, but that's not much use when all you want is to be together in the flesh.

'Bury me in the churchyard,' he said one day, and I agreed that I would, but most of the time we didn't talk about death. We talked about the next hospital appointment, about ways of alleviating the symptoms that were bothering him most and about the advice the consultant was giving. We put the business up for sale, but I had to keep it running in the meantime to fulfil all the bookings we'd taken so that it would be worth buying. I was a quivering wreck, rushing from pig roasts to hospital appointments to home, and sometimes stopping by the horses' field to have a private little weep (but I didn't let go totally because I didn't want John to see me red-eyed).

Once John's daughters were told, they were wonderful, and my kids were as supportive as they could possibly be. Everyone wanted to do something, but there was nothing that could be done. We just had to get through this, surviving one day at a time.

John desperately wanted to stay at home, but by mid-May he was throwing up constantly and in terrible pain, so I got him taken back to hospital where they could at least administer morphine for him. He hated it, saying,

'Get me out of here! This is a guinea-pig ward! They don't know what they're doing!' He was transferred to a Macmillan ward, and still he didn't twig that he had cancer. Possibly it was just as well.

One day I asked a nurse the difficult question, making sure we were out of his hearing: 'How long has he got?'

The answer I got was vague and useless: 'The later they diagnose, the shorter the time.'

In fact we were very close to the end by then. The last couple of weeks flew past. John was not in any pain but he was still not resigned to dying; he was angry and felt cheated of years of his life. As the cancer got into his brain he began to have fits in which he thrashed around, and one of the nurses, Charlie, sat for hours on the edge of his bed, helping to restrain him so he didn't fall out. There was talk of sending him home to die, which was what he would have wanted, but I was terrified that I wouldn't be able to cope if he had a fit when I was home alone with him.

John's last night was very precious to me. I called in the hospital chaplain and he was enormously helpful.

'From what you tell me, John has fitted more into his sixty-four years than many people do in ninety-four. He's had a rich and full life, in which he has given and received great love, not just to you, his daughters and his immediate family, but to a host of wonderful friends.'

I wasn't sure if John could hear and understand what he was saying, but he lay quietly as if listening.

The chaplain continued: 'His memory will live on in everyone who loved him when his spirit passes over to the other side. Now, shall we say a prayer together?'

I closed my eyes and bent my head, hands together, as I used to do at Sunday school when I was a little girl. John and I had always been uneasy bedfellows with organised religion, but this man had said exactly the right things at the time.

At 4 a.m., I sensed he didn't have much longer to go, so I called Emma, who was in Kent, Sam, who was in Brixham, Graham and Helen, and told them all they should come to say goodbye. Sam was the last to arrive, and ten minutes after she got there John took his last breath. Emma was telling us about a magic trick he used to do for her when she was a kid, and then he emitted a death rattle and died. It was only six weeks since his cancer had been diagnosed.

I stayed on my own with him for a long while, and his spirit was so strongly in the room, I could almost feel his arms around me. Afterwards, I went for lunch with the children, the first time I'd eaten in forty-eight hours. Everything seemed unreal. I'd had no time at all to prepare myself – maybe you never can – and it came as a body blow. John had been such a larger-than-life character that it was impossible to imagine life without him. His passing left a huge, unfathomable hole in the universe.

I wasn't the only person who thought so. The hundreds of friends who travelled across the country to be at his funeral all felt the same way. I got through the day in a haze, as if I was on medication (although I wasn't). I'd had a lovely CD made up with all of John's favourite pieces of music on it: our wedding hymns, and then Bette Midler's 'Wind Beneath My Wings'. The ceremony was beautiful and it was followed by a proper wake, which was like a big party, the kind of party John liked to throw – with a pig roast, of course. I kept turning round and expecting to see John laughing and joking in the heart of it.

Two weeks after the funeral we – I was still saying 'we', couldn't stop myself – had a booking to do a pig roast at a wedding for five hundred people. I dragged myself through the day like the sole survivor of a shipwreck, and then I collapsed. I don't remember much about that period, but I had to cancel the rest of the summer bookings for the business. I simply couldn't do it. I remember standing by the fridge keening, the way you see Middle Eastern women keening on the television news. I've got no idea how I got through the next few weeks. It's too painful to remember.

Towards the end John had been offered a place in a hospice in Barnstaple, but by that time he was too poorly to be moved. One day, when I was falling apart, I rang them to ask for their help. I sobbed so hard down the phone that I couldn't breathe, and the woman there put me in touch with a grief counsellor, who helped a little, although all I remember is sobbing my way through each appointment.

That whole period is a blur of grief so raw it was as though my skin had been peeled off. For a long time I genuinely couldn't see how I was going to carry on living without John by my side.

24

Emailing Long Lost Family

I'd had over twenty years with John and, although we'd had our fair share of troubles to contend with, they were fun, happy years full of love and laughter. After he'd gone, once I'd started to get my strength back, I downsized my life, made it simpler. I didn't go back to work but began to volunteer at the local kennels and to help take care of a friend with dementia, while still spending plenty of time with my beloved horses. I visited my grandchildren and took an interest in all their achievements: sports trophies, piano exams, college applications. Helen and Graham were wonderful and often invited me to stay, but they had their own lives to live and couldn't be expected to look after me. I felt very strongly that John's spirit was still with me, but that didn't help much when all I wanted was to cuddle up on the sofa and have a chat with him.

Somehow, bit by bit, I had to achieve the unthinkable and build myself a life without John's physical presence.

And I did it. All those years when I had been the one in the shadows, the peahen to his peacock, I'd been learning lessons about how to be a sociable person. After he had gone I found that a lot of his friends were genuinely my friends as well, and that they got to know me better when he wasn't around, being the centre of attention. I kept myself busy so as to ease the loneliness of being one person instead of half of a couple. It took a lot of getting used to, as everyone who has lost a long-term partner will know, but it can be done.

Sometimes my thoughts were with Sheila, my missing sister, but I couldn't think how to go about tracing her. I wrote once more to Phyllis and Fred Renouf, but this time there was no reply. I supposed that if money had been no obstacle I could have hired a private detective, but it was tight, so I didn't. I sometimes watched the television series *Who Do You Think You Are?*, in which the family histories of celebrities were traced. I paid attention to the methods their research team used – trawling through local newspaper archives, checking registers of births, marriages and deaths – but I had tried most of them already and couldn't think of anything new to try. I bought a computer but never really got my head around how to use it, and then it broke and I didn't bother to get it fixed.

In May 2011, I spotted a new programme entitled *Long Lost Family* in the TV listings. I didn't watch much television as a rule, apart from *Strictly Come Dancing*, which Helen and I were addicted to. (She knew all the dances, of course, and we'd compare notes after every show on what we thought of the dancers.) In *Long Lost Family*, the participants weren't celebrities but normal people, and they were helped to find family members after decades of separation. I knew that Nicky Campbell, one of the presenters, had been adopted and had traced his own birth family, so he was familiar with the kind of emotions the experience can provoke. In an article I read that Davina McCall, the other presenter, had been brought up by her grandparents because her mother was not able to take care of her. It seemed that both would have clear insights into the difficulties of fractured families, and I watched the show with interest.

The techniques they used to track down family members seemed similar to those on *Who Do You Think You Are?*, but *Long Lost Family* had quite a different feel because they were tracing people who were still alive rather than ancestors. Everyone seemed to burst into tears at the point when they were told 'We've found your father', or 'We've traced your daughter'. I remembered the feeling when I got the phone call from Eric saying he'd just spoken to Daisy, my birth mother. I hadn't cried then but I'd been pretty shaken up. And I remembered the crushing disappointment when I got the letter from Dora Noël telling me that my father, Henri Le Gresley, was already dead. I could certainly empathise with these people, and I hoped that their experiences of the new relationships they found would end their lifetime's search, and bring them peace and happiness.

And then came the announcement at the end of the show – 'If you would like us to trace your long-lost family member …' – and the spark of an idea in my head. I rang Helen and told her about it.

'Mum, when are you going to get your computer fixed?' she asked, laughing. 'All right, I'll email them for you.'

A couple of days later, I called Helen to check she had sent the email.

'Yes, it's gone off. I did it the night you asked me to.'

'Is there no reply yet?'

'There was a message saying that they have so many applications it could take a long time, even months, for them to get back to us.'

'Maybe my story is not the kind of thing they're looking for.'

'It's a bit soon to tell, Mum. Give it time.'

A week went by, and then another week.

'Are you sure you sent it to the right email address?' I asked Helen.

'Completely sure. They probably get hundreds, even thousands of emails, and they'll be sifting through them.'

'What did you write?'

Patiently, she told me again the way she had written about my missing sister who'd stayed on Jersey through the war years. It sounded pretty clear.

'Do you think you should send it again, just in case it didn't get through?'

'No, Mum.' I could tell her patience was wearing thin.

Summer came and I spent a lot of time riding along Devon country lanes beside the wildflower verges and hedgerows, through the bluebell woods, or along the coast. I liked the feeling of self-sufficiency that came from riding alone, miles from anywhere. Maybe it's growing up an only child that made me develop a love of solitude and an ability to take care of myself through all the different life experiences I've had. There's got to be a positive side to loneliness.

Summer faded into autumn, and frost was sparkling on the grass when I went to feed the horses in the morning. One day in early December I had been Christmas shopping, then I'd stopped for lunch with a friend, and had done some errands. I didn't even realise I'd left my mobile phone at home until I got back and saw the answering machine blinking away with half-a-dozen messages. My mobile phone showed umpteen missed calls, all of them from Helen. My heart stopped just for an instant, worrying that it might be bad news. I picked up the phone and dialled straight away.

'For goodness sake, Mother, where the hell have you been? I've been trying to get hold of you all day.'

'What's the emergency?'

'Someone from the telly is trying to reach you. From *Long Lost Family*. I've got the number here. You'd better hurry up and get back to them before they decide you're a long-lost cause.' She gave me the number and I scribbled it on the pad by the phone. 'Oh, and Mum?'

'Yes?'

'Don't forget to call me back and tell me what they say.'

25

The Professionals Take Over

My call was answered by a junior researcher at a television-production company called Wall to Wall. She was extremely friendly and we had a long chat about my search for Sheila, in which I answered all her questions as best I could. Although I had trouble remembering the order in which things had happened, I could describe it all to her quite clearly, from the cup of tea at the Renoufs' to the last time I saw Daisy in Leeds. I had lots of birth certificates, letters, photographs and the 'document' Daisy had written for me about her past. She was particularly interested to hear that Sheila had spent the war years in Jersey and hoped there might be some records that would help them to track her down.

'I don't want you to get your hopes up,' she cautioned. 'We are only able to take on a small fraction of the cases we are emailed about. I was just ringing you to clarify a few details, but no decision has been made about whether we will be able to take on your search.'

'OK,' I said. 'When do you think you might decide?'

'We're starting to film the next series early in the New Year so you will know one way or another pretty soon.'

'I'm moving home on 2 January,' I told her. I'd decided to move into a little one-bed retirement home, which I thought would be easy to manage because I'd finally had to admit I was having trouble carrying the coal up the steps to my cottage, and wheeling the logs round the back in a wheelbarrow. I gave her the new address and my mobile number.

Straight after Christmas, I got another phone call from the researcher, wondering if she could have a look at the key documents, especially the birth and adoption certificates, so between them, Graham and Helen scanned and sent them to her. (Lots of my documents were stored in boxes in Graham's garage from previous moves.)

A few weeks later a woman called Louise phoned. 'I'm delighted to tell you that we are going to take on your search,' she said. 'There are no guarantees that we will find Sheila, of course, but we'll give it a try.'

'Oh, that's wonderful! Thank you so much!' It was a lovely feeling to know that someone else was going to look into my background on my behalf.

'I'd like to come down to Devon to meet you and get more of the information we need,' she explained.

I said that was fine. 'Don't wear any decent clothes, though,' I warned. 'I've got horses and dogs.'

'You have? That's wonderful! I love horses.'

I met Louise on 6 March at Eggesford station, a tiny rural stop on the single-track Tarka Line, with chugging trains that are like funny old buses. We went out to meet the horses first and bonded over our shared love of all things equestrian. Next, she came back to my tiny house and we talked through my complex family history over a cup of tea. As I'd predicted, she soon got dog hair and mucky paw prints all over her jeans.

'What proportion of the searches you start end up being on the telly?' I asked.

She explained: 'I don't know the exact figures, but there are a lot we start then can't go forward with for one reason or another. I know it's hard for you to hang on …'

'Don't worry about me. I'm tough as old boots,' I told her. 'I've had to be.'

I didn't particularly think they would succeed in finding Sheila. I just thought it would be interesting to let the experts have a try after I'd been floundering about for nearly three decades in my own very amateurish style. It seemed so unlikely after all this time that I resolutely refused to get my hopes up and just carried on with my normal life without dwelling on it too much. Besides, even if they did find Sheila by some fluke, I had no idea what kind of person she might be; perhaps she was intensely private and would hate the idea of being on television. I hoped she would understand that this was the only option I had left to try to find her. Perhaps we would find we had nothing in common and would meet, exchange polite greetings and then go back to our own lives. Or perhaps they wouldn't find her at all.

When Louise left, she promised I would hear from her again soon, and sure enough there was another call a week later. 'Can we come to you on 21 March?' she asked. 'We want to introduce you to Davina McCall.'

That sounded exciting; I wondered if they had found something, but there was no clue from Louise's tone of voice. Whatever happened, I looked forward to meeting Davina because I'd always thought she seemed like such a normal, 'un-starry' type of celeb. She seemed like the kind of person you'd want to be friends with. I rang Helen to tell her.

'What are you going to wear, Mum?'

'Oh, you know me. I'll pull something out of the cupboard.'

'Whatever it is, just make sure it doesn't have dog hair all over it.'

26

A Visit from Davina

I dressed that morning of 21 March in blue trousers and an ivory sweater and wrapped a bright red and purple floral scarf round my neck. The camera crew arrived early and busied themselves with setting up their equipment, both inside and outside the house because they wanted to film Davina arriving. Helen drove up and soon became part of the action when the team filmed us through the kitchen window having a cup of tea and a chat.

There was a buzz of anticipation about Davina's arrival. It was good to keep busy so I wasn't thinking too much about the filming, because then I'd probably have got nervous.

The doorbell rang and cameras were rolling as I opened the front door to see that friendly, familiar face we all know from our television screens smiling broadly at me. Davina was dressed in jeans and a sweater, with hardly any make-up, and looked so natural and 'real' that I immediately felt as though I'd known her for ages. She greeted me like an old friend and gave me her full attention as we made our way into the sitting room and sat side by side on my green-and-white patterned sofa. ('It's a very photogenic sofa,' the cameraman had told me as he trundled it across the room so that it was in front of the window.)

Davina and I chatted for about five minutes. She talked a little about some of the methods they'd tried and said, 'Your search, your story, has been quite a complicated one and has thrown up numerous problems. Knowing how much it means to you, it's meant a lot to us to take it on and see if we can help you.'

That was nice. As I listened, I was thinking, '*Gosh, she's got really good skin. She's very pretty.*'

Then suddenly, she said, 'I've got news for you: we've found your sister.'

It came out of the blue and caught me completely unawares. I stuttered like an idiot: 'Oh ... You've found her ...? That is ... won ... it's amazing. You've actually found her ...? I ... can't believe it.'

I was simply stunned. In retrospect I'm amazed I managed not to use any swear words. I'd been looking for Sheila for so long that I really hadn't thought they'd find her.

'Would you like to see a picture of her?' Davina asked. She reached into her jacket pocket.

The photo showed an attractive silver-haired woman smiling against a backdrop of some kind of garden. 'She looks like my mum,' I said straight away. 'Oh, it's absolutely wonderful.'

'This is slightly bittersweet,' Davina continued, her eyes never leaving my face, 'because Sheila doesn't think she is your full sister.'

'Doesn't she?' I was astounded. How could Daisy not have told me that? Perhaps Sheila had been illegitimate and Daisy was embarrassed to admit it. That must be the explanation. But who was her father?

'We did more digging and came up with something quite incredible,' Davina continued.

'What's that?'

'We found that you have another sister, a full sister.'

Now *that* was a total surprise. 'A full sister?' I stuttered. 'What's she called?'

'She's called Val.'

I felt such a rush of pure happiness that I was speechless. I covered my mouth with my hand, trying in typical fashion to mask my emotions. 'I've got two sisters! I don't know what to say.'

Davina showed me a photograph of Val and it nearly took my breath away.

'Oh, my giddy aunt. That's me! Look at that!' The resemblance was extraordinary. We could have been twins.

Davina hugged me, which was lovely, as I was very close to tears at that point. I'd warned Louise that I wasn't the crying type and if they wanted tears they'd be disappointed, and she had said it didn't matter how I reacted, just to be myself. But in fact, I did have to wipe my eyes a few times.

'Where is Val?' I gasped.

Davina told me she lived in Spain, and explained that they had only found out about her when talking to Sheila the previous week. Sheila remembered that when Daisy left Jersey in 1940 she had been around seven or eight months pregnant. Well, I wasn't born until 1943, so there was no way that child could have been me. The *Long Lost Family* researchers searched for Val's birth record, using Daisy's surname. They found the birth of a child with that name around the right time in Lancashire. Knowing that lots of evacuees ended up in Lancashire, it seemed plausible that Daisy could have ended up giving birth there. Val's birth certificate was ordered and it had the correct mother's name. Because Valerie had been adopted, *Long Lost Family* used a specialist adoption intermediary, legally entitled to find out her new name. The intermediary accessed Val's new name and contacted her.

'How did you find Sheila?' I asked.

Davina explained that their researchers had searched electoral rolls and birth, marriage and death records to track her down. It helped that Sheila's daughters had been creating their own family tree and searching for information online also.

'Sheila has daughters?' I was in a daze. 'Does she want to meet me?

'They are *both* dying to meet you,' Davina said. 'I've got letters they've written to you.'

She brought out Sheila's letter first. It was handwritten on a little notecard and just said she was very happy that I had got in contact, that she had always wondered if I would, and she said that she looked forward to meeting me. She added that she was a widow, with four daughters and lived near Portsmouth.

Then Davina showed me Val's letter. It was typed out – like an official letter, I thought. She began by saying, 'Hello, what a surprise!' then told me a little about her life: she had worked as a civil servant, had a husband and two sons, and they had retired to Spain, where they loved entertaining, especially having parties round their pool. She sounded very lively and bubbly – just my kind of person.

'It's amazing. I've got two sisters.' I kept repeating it, as if the repetition would make it feel real, but in fact nothing about the day felt real. I was sitting on my sofa talking to one of the most famous women on British television while a camera crew filmed us, so it was hardly an average day for starters – and now this!

'Can I tell Helen?' I asked, and when they said yes, I rushed through to the kitchen to break the news. She was ecstatic on my behalf.

'Oh, Mum, that's brilliant! When can we meet them?' She was jumping up and down and hugging me in excitement.

'We're still making the arrangements, but we're hoping to do it sometime next week,' Louise told us.

So soon! 'But will Val be able to come over from Spain?'

'Yes, don't worry. We'll make sure she's there.'

'Are you sure they are happy to be part of the programme?' I asked. 'I don't want them to feel they're being forced into anything.'

'No, we wouldn't do it if they weren't both happy.'

I retreated inside myself a bit at that stage. It's always taken me ages to process emotional situations, and this was about as emotional as it got. Davina stayed chatting to us for a while – I think she was just checking I was all right. The whole team were very solicitous. Inside my head, the words were churning around: *I've got two sisters, I've got two sisters.*

Eventually, the crew began to put my living room back the way it had been before. Davina said goodbye, adding that she would see me the following week, and gave me another huge hug before setting off in her car. The others left a bit later, after making sure my house was in pristine condition (much tidier than it had been before, if truth be told).

After Helen went home that evening, I looked for the remote control to switch on the telly, but couldn't find it. I didn't really want to watch telly anyway. I just wanted to sit and think and reread those lovely letters from my sisters and examine every detail of their photos. (The remote turned up several days later; I think Davina must have been sitting on it because it was jammed right down between the cushions on her side of the sofa.)

As I went to bed that night, still in a complete daze, I thought that there was only one thing that would have made the day more perfect. If only John had been there to share it with me. He was the one who knew better than anyone else how much the search for my sister had meant to me, and he would have shared my joy at this amazing development as no one else could.

27

The Meeting at High Wycombe

Over the next few days, I couldn't think about anything except the forthcoming meeting with my sisters. There were so many questions I wanted to ask that I didn't know where to start.

Had Sheila known about us both? I couldn't remember exactly what Davina had told me – my brain was scrambled – but I was sure she'd said that Val had been adopted and knew nothing of her birth family. The team had only got in touch with her the week before, so she would still be in a state of shock to find she had two new sisters – as I was too.

Louise rang to confirm that the meeting would be on 26 March at a hotel in High Wycombe called Danesfield House. She said it was traditional to choose somewhere near where the person who initiated the search was born, so that's why High Wycombe was chosen. Danesfield House had beautiful grounds and the team were crossing their fingers that the weather would allow us to film outdoors. And she said that I could bring Graham, Helen and their partners and children along to the hotel so that the extended families could meet each other.

Helen helped me to shop for a new outfit: some smart black trousers, a turquoise-blue top and purply blue jacket, with one of my trademark floral scarves. I don't do dresses and it's a very rare occasion indeed when I'm seen in a skirt! Helen and I travelled to High Wycombe on the evening of 25 March and stayed in a lovely hotel run by an Indian family. They offered us a choice of English or Indian food for breakfast, and I love curries so I was momentarily tempted, but I decided it wasn't a great idea when I was shortly going to be breathing on my new-found sisters, so I stuck to toast and marmalade.

'You seem really calm, Mum. Are you sure you're OK?' Helen asked.

'I'm fine.'

And I *was* completely calm at that stage. I think the reality hadn't struck home for me yet. It just seemed like a lovely trip away from home. I got ready, putting on a lick of make-up and asking Helen, 'Is it all in the right place?' (I don't normally wear any) then trying to style my hair into semi-neatness.

Davina came to collect me from the hotel at ten o'clock. I gave Helen a goodbye hug then set off in Davina's car with her. The weather was incredible: bright sun and virtually cloudless blue skies, like a day in July rather than late March.

'It's such a big day for you, isn't it?' Davina asked.

'It's been so long – so long,' I said. 'It's like stepping off the edge into the complete unknown.'

'You're remarkably calm, considering.'

I laughed. 'Yes, everyone keeps telling me that.'

'You told me before that you have difficulty expressing your emotions, but you certainly seemed quite overcome with emotion when I brought you the news about your sisters last week.' She turned and smiled at me.

'That was an exceptional situation, you have to admit. At my age, it's not every day that you hear you've got two new sisters …'

We drove through an archway into the forecourt of Danesfield House, and I could see straight away how grand it was. There were battlements, Tudor-style chimneys and square towers, all painted white with a red tiled roof. The footmen wore smart liveries and every surface was gleaming with furniture polish. We walked out into the grounds, which were immaculately kept and stretched right down to the River Thames in the distance. Daffodils were flowering in clusters around the lawn and the trees were in bud. It was simply gorgeous. I kept glancing around, wondering if Sheila and Val were there yet, but there was no sign of them, so perhaps I was the first to arrive.

'*What if they change their minds and don't come?*' I worried, but reassured myself that surely they wouldn't drop out at such a late stage. Val must already have flown over from Spain.

Louise was there, as usual rushing around, organising everyone else. Davina and I were directed to a wood and stone bench looking out across the Thames Valley, and the cameras were set up around us. It seemed that this was where all the action was going to take place.

'I'm going to leave you now,' Davina said with a smile and gave me a hug.

'They'll be coming in a minute,' Louise told me. She offered me some water but I said I was fine.

Up above, I noticed some red kites circling. They're a beautiful bird of prey with a reddish-brown body and a forked tail. We don't get them down in Devon, so I was fascinated to watch them swooping and soaring high in the sky. I think I was lulled into a kind of trance. It was too hot in my jacket and scarf, but I didn't want to take them off because I wouldn't look so well turned-out. It really was like a summer's day.

'They're coming,' someone hissed, and all of a sudden

the enormity of the situation hit me and I panicked. I used to be like that when I sat exams at school: calm and almost indifferent until I was in the hall turning the exam paper over, and then I'd come out in a cold sweat. Now I had no idea which direction my sisters would be arriving from, if they'd come together, or, if they came separately, which one I should run to first. I felt shaky, excited and terrified at the same time.

As it happened, I saw Val first, wearing an elegant pale-green trouser suit. I knew it was her from the photo, but even if I hadn't seen a picture I would have known anyway, because we were so alike it was like watching myself walking towards me. I started walking in her direction, but the little kitten heels of my boots sank down into the grass and I had to balance on the balls of my feet. We just grinned and threw our arms round each other. I saw Sheila coming from the other direction, in a lovely fuchsia top and dark grey trousers. She joined us for a hug, saying, 'Lovely to meet you,' in a voice that sounded much calmer than I felt. I think I said, 'Oh, how wonderful! I've got sisters!' and Val said, 'It is, absolutely!'

When I'd composed myself, we sat down on the bench together. We linked hands and at first we just remarked on our family likeness. I couldn't stop grinning.

Sheila said, 'I can't believe how alike you two are. You look like your mum.'

I told her, 'I think *you* look like your mum.' They were both very attractive women.

Val nodded towards our linked hands: 'Look, we've all got the same nails.' I remembered Daisy telling me that nice hands ran in the family, all the way from her old grandmother who did manual work and yet had very beautiful hands. My daughter and my granddaughters have them as well.

Sheila, Val and I had so much to talk about that it was hard to find a place to start. 'Wouldn't it have been lovely if we'd all grown up together?' I suggested. 'Imagine the mischief we'd have got up to.'

'I'm the eldest so I'd have got my way,' Sheila said. 'I've waited seventy-odd years to be bossy.' Val and I looked at each other with a glint in our eyes. I knew she was thinking the same as me: that we would never have let Sheila boss us around.

I was beginning to relax a little because I could tell Sheila and Val were both intelligent, friendly women. It felt as if we'd known each other for ages rather than just meeting five minutes ago. I was keen to bond with them, and that's not something that can be artificially manufactured – it's either there or it's not – but all the signs were good.

Louise suggested that we might like to walk up to the hotel patio for a drink, and we jumped to our feet, thinking that it sounded like a great idea. The crew filmed us walking up the steps, arms round each other's waists, and the only thing they couldn't see was that my microphone was falling out of my trouser pocket under my jacket at the back. I didn't like to ask everyone to stop while I fixed it so I just walked carefully, trying not to dislodge it any further.

Once we were seated at a little table, a waiter came and asked what we wanted to drink, and the three of us, I swear to God, said, 'Gin and tonic, please,' in perfect unison. We burst out laughing. It was obviously one more thing we had in common.

The conversation was fractured at first, as we talked about where we'd stayed the night before and how each of us felt about taking part in the programme. Val was the most shaken up of the three of us.

'I only found out I was adopted when my father died back in 1978,' Val said. 'My parents didn't tell me when I was a child. And I only heard about you two last week when I got a call from a researcher – then Nicky Campbell flew out to tell me about you.'

'Gosh, that must be a lot to take on board,' I sympathised. 'I already knew about Sheila's existence but I didn't have the faintest clue about you until six days ago. I met our mother, Daisy, but she never told me she'd had another child. Did she tell you, Sheila?'

'I knew there were two children born during the war, both girls,' Sheila said, 'but Daisy told us they had been killed in an air raid.'

Val and I both gasped.

'She said *what*?' To say I was shocked would be an understatement.

'When did you last see Daisy?' Sheila asked me.

It was an awkward moment. 'I'm not sure if you know that Daisy died around twenty years ago. I went to her funeral. The Bartons said they didn't know how to contact you.'

'Yes, the *Long Lost Family* researcher told me she had died.' She didn't sound very upset about it and I wondered what was behind the rift in their relationship, but now wasn't the time to ask.

'If you thought Val and I had been killed in an air raid, you must have been astonished when the team contacted you to say I was alive and searching for you.'

'Yes and no,' Sheila said. 'I believed Daisy at the time, but later I heard my Aunt Joyce telling Mum that you were still alive but had been adopted. There was nothing I could have done to try to find you, but I did wonder if I'd hear from you one day.'

'I hope you don't mind that I used a television programme to find you both,' I said. 'I had tried everything else I could think of.'

'I must admit, I was a little bit dubious at the start,' Sheila said. 'I wasn't sure when they approached me. It does drag up lots of memories – some good, some not so good. But when I heard you'd been looking for me for thirty years, I decided that it wasn't fair on you not to take part.'

'Aww,' I hugged her. 'I wouldn't have minded if you didn't want to, so long as we could all get together. But we'd never have found Val without their help.'

'That's true. We didn't even have a starting point. Goodness knows how they tracked you down in Spain, Val. Their researchers certainly know their job.'

We compared the number of children we each had and showed photos on our phones, remarking on the family resemblances of the next generation. We talked about the jobs we'd done: Val had worked at the MOD for a while, and Sheila had been a waitress before she got married but hadn't worked since then, too busy raising her girls. She'd been widowed twice and her last husband, Ivor, had died around the same time I lost John. I could tell by the wobble in her voice that she still missed him terribly. Val was the lucky one of the three of us: she was still with Pete, the husband she had married back at the age of eighteen.

It wasn't a deep conversation by any means – we had to cover the bases first – but I was beginning to get a sense of their characters. Val's quite a down-to-earth person who calls a spade a spade, while Sheila's outlook on the world is calm and coloured by her religious beliefs. She had a strict Catholic upbringing and converted to become a Jehovah's Witness when she married Ivor. I was slightly wary of this religion after my experiences of Billie, my stepmother, trying to convert all the neighbours wherever she lived, and judging everybody by the standards of her church, but I soon realised that wasn't Sheila's way. She seemed very serene and self-contained.

When the drinks were finished Louise came over to ask if we were ready to go back and rejoin our families. She explained that our luggage would be moved into the hotel where Val was staying, and that dinner would take place there that evening. We rose to go our separate ways for now, with fresh hugs, reluctant to part even for a couple of hours now that we'd found each other at last.

'I hope we'll see a lot of each other,' Val said to us. 'We've got to make up for lost time.'

Before we left Danesfield House, Louise asked me to do one more interview, in which I'd explain what it meant for me to have found my sisters. I think my head was spinning from the effects of the gin and tonic, as well as the excitement of the day, when I told her, beaming from ear to ear: 'I feel free for the first time in my whole lifetime. It's just wonderful!'

28

The Families
Get Together

When Sheila, Val and I arrived at the hotel where we were having dinner, we found our families had already got acquainted with each other. During the day, while we were filming at Danesfield House, they'd been introducing themselves and swapping life stories, so that by evening they almost knew more about each other than we did. Graham and Fiona had arrived, along with their children Meghan and Jacob, and Helen was there with Hannah and her son Joe, who was just eight years old. Val's husband Pete was smiling away, along with their son Mick and Mick's daughter Kerry. And Sheila's youngest daughter, Penny, was there too.

When I walked in, with butterflies in my tummy, Penny broke the ice by coming straight over to say, 'Hello, Auntie Cherry!' She was a lovely, affectionate girl – in her early forties, I guessed, but that's still a girl to me! Sheila had told me that Penny was keen on researching the family history, and I asked her how she was getting on with it.

'The Banks are a complicated lot,' she said. 'We'll have to draw a family tree someday to try to make sense of it all.'

Val's husband Pete took one look at me standing beside Val and slapped his head. 'Oh my God, there are two of you now!' he said in a tone that implied he wasn't quite sure how he was going to cope. Straight away I warmed to him; he obviously had an irreverent and humorous take on the world.

I was introduced to Val's son Mick, who was the spitting image of Pete, and then her granddaughter Kerry, who reminded me of Helen.

'My husband Eugene's at home, looking after our little ones,' she told me.

'Wow! Val's a great-grandmother! She looks so young and glamorous, you'd never believe it.' The whole thing was overwhelming, and I was constantly aware that this was a once-in-a-lifetime experience. History was being made in our extended families.

Before we sat down to eat, the *Long Lost Family* team came in to say goodbye. They were leaving us to get acquainted in private now. I hugged everyone and thanked them from the bottom of my heart.

'Wasn't it a perfect day for a reunion?' Louise commented. 'Only trouble is, I got sunburned standing out there for so long! Who would think to wear sunscreen in March?' I had to admit, her nose and forehead did look a little pink.

'None of this would have been possible without you,' I told her. Looking round the room, I still couldn't believe that all these people were members of my family. It was the most wonderful gift imaginable.

When we sat down to dinner, Sheila, Val and I made sure we were close to each other so we could carry on talking, but there was no opportunity to have a serious conversation above the noise and excitement. It was all I could do to try to memorise everybody's names – a task made doubly hard because people kept changing places at the table so they all got a chance to talk to everyone else.

'I really want to hear more about the family in Jersey,' I told Sheila. 'Could we get together soon?'

'You're in Devon, aren't you?' she said. 'Why don't I come down to you for a visit and bring the family albums? It's perhaps easiest to follow the relationships when you've got pictures in front of you.'

'Oh, yes please!' I said, clapping my hands together. 'I'd love that! Val, do you want to come as well? I've only got a little place but we could all squeeze in.'

'I hate coming back to Britain,' Val said. 'It's too cold. You two will have to come out to Spain to stay with Pete and me.'

Sheila and I looked at each other. 'Absolutely!' I said. 'Just name the date and I'll be there.'

I can't remember what we ate that night. I do recall that the drinks flowed freely. And then, at around eleven o'clock, Sheila established her bossy eldest sister credentials by announcing loudly, 'Party's over, everyone. I think we should all go to bed now.' Astonishingly, we stood up and began to filter out. I think we were exhausted from the emotional highs of the day, but there was definitely a sense that we let Sheila be the boss – for that one night at least. Upstairs in my hotel room, I was asleep before my head hit the pillow.

The next morning, all three extended families crowded into the breakfast room. Ignoring the buffet, we circled round, swapping phone numbers and addresses, while the younger generations 'friended' each other on Facebook. And then it was time to go our separate ways: Sheila to Hampshire, Val and Pete to Heathrow to catch a flight to Alicante, and me back down to my little house in Devon.

I gazed out the train window at the passing countryside and mentally pinched myself. Did that really just happen? Did I really just meet my two sisters? And not only did I meet them, but I felt an instant connection with them.

All three of us had had very different life experiences, but we seemed like kindred spirits and I hoped the bond we had begun to forge would last for the rest of our lives. It certainly felt as though it might.

The day after I got back to Devon, I was on the phone to Val and Sheila just to check they'd had a safe journey home. We had a natter, reliving the events of the previous day. It had flown past in a flash, and I wanted to set all the details in memory and not lose any of them. Sheila and I looked at our diaries and discussed arranging a date when she would come down to Devon. I was impatient to do it as soon as possible, but she had a busy life so it looked as though it was going to have to be early summer.

In the meantime, the three of us fell into a habit of talking regularly on the phone. Sheila and Val Skyped each other, and Sheila tried to talk me into fixing my old computer so I could Skype as well, but I decided I was happy enough with chatting on a landline. Technology is not my forte. We talked about odd bits and pieces but the conversation was more focused on our lives in the present than the past. I wanted to wait until Sheila came to stay to ask her for the full story of her background and her life with Daisy. It was extraordinary how different our childhoods sounded despite the fact that we'd had the same mother. All I knew about Sheila's past at that point came from the document Daisy had written for me.

A few weeks after the meeting at Danesfield House, Wall to Wall sent me a DVD of the programme they were planning to show. Sheila and Val got one as well. My hands were shaking as I slipped it into the DVD player and sat down to watch. I couldn't bear to look at myself on screen; vanity, I know, but I thought I looked really old in the close-ups, not the way I think of myself at all. I called Helen over to watch it and she was disappointed that they hadn't used the clip of her reaction when I went in to tell her they'd found Sheila, but she thought the programme was riveting. Sheila and Val both looked great, and I was amused to see how well our outfits coordinated; you might almost have thought we'd discussed them in advance (we hadn't, of course). I loved the way they had cut old black-and-white footage of goose-stepping Nazis in Jersey through the bits about Sheila's childhood there. She obviously had strong memories of the occupation, and I looked forward to asking her all about it.

There hadn't been much time to question Val about her childhood, but I learned from the programme that she'd been born in Lancashire, and that Daisy had given her up for adoption when she was just nine days old. Her birth name was Beryl Marguerite Knowle – she had the same middle name as Sheila – but it was quite different from the name Val Wells by which she was now known.

I've got no idea how the researchers managed to track her down, and to do it as quickly as they did, but hats off to them!

We'd been told that we could ask for changes if there was anything incorrect, but I was quite happy with the programme. It captured the spirit of our meeting in High Wycombe perfectly, and showed the genuine affection we felt for each other right from the start. You would never think those three woman sitting on a bench at Danesfield House were meeting for the first time. There's a tangible connection between us that comes across on screen.

I watched the programme again when it aired in May 2012, and lots of friends and family members got in touch to say how moving they found it. I had no regrets at all about getting Helen to send that email: if I hadn't, I'd never have found Sheila and I'd never even have known about Val. How sad it would have been if we had gone to our graves without getting to know each other.

29

My Jersey Family's Wartime History

Penny and her husband drove Sheila down to visit me in summer 2012, and I was delighted to welcome them to my little home with a cup of tea and some homemade cherry and almond cake. Although in reality we barely knew each other, it felt like greeting friends of some years standing rather than people I'd only met once before. After Penny left, Sheila and I started chatting about our shared family history and hardly stopped over the next few days, except when I went off to see to the horses and dogs first thing in the morning and at the end of the day. During the rest of the time we toured the sights of the local area – going to a garden centre, to Barnstaple – but most of all we talked, right from the evening she first arrived.

'Daisy always led me to believe that Henri Le Gresley Noël was your father,' I told her. 'I even put adverts in

Jersey and Southampton local newspapers looking for "Sheila Marguerite Noël", but I realise I was way off-track.'

'No, my birth father was a man called Mr Gibbons. I don't even know his Christian name. He's not named on my birth certificate and he disappeared when I was a baby – before he could be called upon to pay to support his child. All I know about him is that he went to La Salle Jesuit College in Jersey. I believe Daisy brought me up for the first nine months then handed me over to my grandparents, whom I called Mum and Dad. All my childhood memories are of them and my uncle Bernard, who was three-and-a-half years older so more like a brother than an uncle.' Sheila was very articulate, choosing her words with care.

'There were two other siblings, were there not?'

'Aunt Joyce and Uncle William were evacuated to Rochdale with Daisy in 1940. I remember waving as their boat pulled away from the harbour. We should have been on that boat but Granny didn't want to leave Granddad, and he didn't want to go because he wasn't certain he'd be able to find a job on the mainland.'

'Daisy told me he worked as an assistant veterinary surgeon.'

Sheila frowned. 'No, that's not right. He had a job on Jersey, delivering goods round the island on his horse and cart. It was a big shire horse.'

I wondered if I was misremembering Daisy's letter. I certainly remembered her mentioning shire horses. 'What kind of stuff did he deliver?'

'You probably know that Jersey is renowned for its beautiful gardens … he transported garden tools and supplies, such as lawnmowers. That was one thing. During the war he carried all sorts, whatever he was asked to.'

I shifted on the sofa, fascinated by this crucial part of my family's history. 'What was it like during the occupation? I heard there were terrible food shortages.'

'Well, my grandmother was quite a plump French lady who weighed sixteen stone at the start of the war, and she was down to six stone by the end. After the Normandy landings, no food was getting through except for Red Cross parcels, so the Germans were starving as well.'

'Daisy told me that her father was in a concentration camp and lost a lot of weight there. She said he went down from fifteen stone to five stone.'

Sheila shook her head. 'That's not true. I'm afraid you need to take anything Daisy told you with a pinch of salt.'

'He wasn't even in a camp?' I was astounded. Had she simply invented that, or had she got the wrong impression from something that was said after the war?

'No, he wasn't. He fought in the First World War with the Jersey militia, but during the Second World War he stayed with us on the island. By his late forties he was a sick man from injuries sustained in the first war, and he died at the age of fifty-two.'

'Oh, I'm sorry.' I reached across to touch her shoulder but Sheila was quite composed. It had happened a long time ago. 'What was it like, being there with Germans marching up and down the streets?'

'It was hard. We lived in fear: fear that we might be taken to a camp in Germany; fear that our neighbours might be collaborators waiting to spy on us. "Don't say anything," Mum kept repeating. Dad had a crystal set up in the loft and she was petrified it would get us all arrested. He'd come in from work, lay some newspaper on the kitchen table, climb up to stand on it then stick his head through the hatch into the loft to listen to the BBC News. We kept hearing about people being arrested and deported for having radio sets, and Mum eventually got it down and smashed it up. I remember her saying to him, "What about the children? What about the children?" There was a German anti-aircraft firing range just at the back of our house in Bellozanne Valley and they were driving past all the time, so she had good reason to be scared.'

'Your dad sounds like a bit of a rebel ...' *Good for him!* I thought, although at the same time I could fully understand why her mum had smashed the radio to protect her family.

'He hated the Germans violently and there were many occasions when he could have been taken away. If any Germans were coming towards you, you were supposed to get off the pavement to let them past, but he never would. He used to stand there and spit at their feet, and usually they'd step down and walk around him. They didn't really want any trouble with islanders if they could avoid it. Hitler was pleased he had a piece of British territory and he wanted to behave like a gentleman to the British, but it didn't stop us having this terrible fear. I remember watching the Germans goose-stepping everywhere and feeling really, really scared.'

'Did you start school during the occupation?'

'Yes, Bernard and I were at school. But then I caught diphtheria and was carted off to the isolation hospital. I was told I could take one toy with me so I chose my favourite little toy dog. What I didn't realise was that I wouldn't be able to bring it out with me again in case it spread germs. When I found out, I cried and cried.' Sheila smiled wryly at the memory. 'I wore *sabots* – clogs with wooden soles and canvas tops. Dad used to hammer hobnails through the soles to stop them wearing out so quickly, but one of them came through the heel of my *sabot*. When I was discharged from hospital I couldn't walk because of that nail digging in my heel, and Mum and Bernard had to carry me down the road between them.' She shook her head, still smiling.

'Do you have any photos from that period?' She'd said she was bringing some photo albums along with her and I was looking forward to putting faces to all these people.

'No, I don't have any from during the war. We were too poor to have a camera then, and afterwards Dad was too ill to work and we were living on his state pension of two pounds, ten shillings and ten pence. But I'll show you what I do have.'

She fetched a photograph album from her suitcase and began to point out characters to me. 'That's Dad – our granddad. And that's Mum. She was a very loving woman who had to watch her children going through some heart-breaking experiences.'

I looked at the couple on whose grave I had placed flowers when I went to Jersey with Eric, and felt a connection with them. 'They must have been beside themselves with worry about their three children over in Britain. Did you hear anything from them during the war?'

'No, not until 1944 when we started to get letters through the Red Cross. It was only then we found out that Bill had lied about his age to enlist. He made it through the war but was killed while on demob leave in Aldershot in 1946.'

'Oh, my God! What happened?' I remembered Daisy

telling me he'd been killed by the Germans but she didn't go into detail.

'Some soldier got belligerent and pushed him. He fell to the ground and hit his head, and the doctors said he had an abnormally thin skull, which fractured. He never regained consciousness. He was only nineteen.'

So it wasn't the Germans: I wondered why Daisy had told me that. Perhaps it was easier to blame the Germans for Bill's death than to accept it as a tragic but random incident. 'That's horrible! How awful for you all!' I hoped it wasn't too difficult for Sheila to talk to me about all these old memories. She was speaking in quite a matter-of-fact tone and her expression was neutral, but it must be hard to relive these sad days.

We focused on the photographs for a while longer and she showed me images of Joyce, Bernard, a much younger version of Daisy than I had known and a host of other relatives whose names I knew I would never remember. Sheila was quite the expert on the extended Banks and Renouf families on the Channel Islands, and told me that she had recently tracked down a relative on Sark after seeing her on a television programme about the island.

I decided it was time for me to start preparing the dinner, so Sheila followed me through to the kitchen and we chatted while I chopped vegetables and checked on the chicken I was roasting. It was only when we were eating that we went back to discussing the family history, after Sheila admired a photograph of Helen dancing, which I had on display.

'I hear that Daisy was something of a dancer in her day,' I said. 'She told me she won prizes for ballroom dancing on the continent.'

'That's all nonsense,' Sheila laughed. 'Did she really tell you that?'

'Yes, in a letter.' I was beginning to wonder if I could believe anything Daisy had told me. Why say she was a dancer if she wasn't? I suppose she was trying to establish a connection with us.

'It's such a shame. I could have met you way back in 1986. All those years, there are plenty of times I could really have used a sister … But at least I've got you and Val now. I can't tell you how much it means to me. Really, I can't.'

Looking at Sheila sitting across my dining room table, with her calm grace, I felt myself fill up with joy that at long last I'd found my missing sister. I'd often dreamed of this moment in the years when I was searching for her, but the reality was more wonderful than anything I could ever have imagined. It was as if a cloud had lifted. I could feel myself rooted in the earth, part of a family that stretched way back through generations, all of them with shared DNA in their cells. It's hard to describe, but it rounded out my sense of self and made me feel more connected to the universe. It was still early days but I already knew it was going to change me fundamentally.

30

Learning more about My Birth Mother

After dinner we went back through to the sitting room and Sheila continued with the story of her early years.

'I can remember the liberation of the island in 1945,' she told me. 'Some Allied landing craft came into the harbour at St Helier and the Germans were rounded up. Everyone was throwing their German marks into the air and trampling on them because we had no way of spending marks anymore.'

'That period must have been so exciting after the years of fear and dread.' I was too young to remember VE Day, but Pop had told me about the ships' horns sounding and everyone dancing in the street.

'Yes, it was. Mum was keen to be reunited with her children as soon as possible, but Joyce had a young family by that stage so she couldn't travel and Bill was still in the army. Daisy came over on a Red Cross boat as soon as she could, and that's when she told us about her two children – and her husband – having been killed in an air raid. She was wearing an ATS uniform.'

I curled my feet underneath me in the chair. 'She wrote to me that she lived in a flat above your mum and dad and that you used to spend part of the time with her and part with them.'

'There's some truth in that,' Sheila said. 'Mum and Dad sold our bungalow in Bellozanne Valley to move to England to be close to their children. They came over on a trip but it didn't work out for various reasons, and on their return they rented a garden flat in St Helier. Daisy and her chap Harold had a room above but I never lived with them. Did she tell you about Harold?'

'Yes. She said he was the love of her life and that he died when they had only been married for six months.'

'Yes, that's correct. I remember Harold, and I believe they were married. After he died Daisy went backwards and forwards between England and Jersey. She took me to England on one occasion then sent me back without paying the fare on the boat. I was supposed to lie that I'd lost my ticket so that Mum would pay at the other end!' Sheila laughed, shaking her head at the notion.

I was beginning to think that nothing would surprise

me now. Daisy sounded as though she'd been very flighty and self-centred back in her twenties. 'She wrote that she brought you over to a special school in Southampton because you had a particularly high IQ.'

'That was just for a couple of terms,' Sheila said. 'Daisy was working in a domestic appointment, looking after a disabled woman and her husband. I really didn't want to be dragged away from all my family and friends, but at least it wasn't too long before my mum – our grandmother, I mean – got me into the intermediate grammar school back on Jersey, which is where I finished my education.'

'Daisy said you came back because you didn't want to live with her and Pete Barton.'

Sheila seemed upset at this. 'I know Daisy said things like that, and to be honest it really hurt me. Daisy also claimed that I was jealous of her relationship with Pete, and nothing could be further from the truth. Why should I be? I'd never looked on Daisy as a mother anyway. After I left school, she insisted I went to live with her and Pete at Catterick Camp in Yorkshire – he'd joined the army – and I was really unhappy there. I escaped by going out a lot to the pictures or going dancing, and at the age of seventeen I got married.'

'Wow! That's very young to marry. I was twenty-one at my first marriage and I thought that was too young.' A thought struck me. 'Did Daisy come to your wedding?'

Sheila shook her head emphatically. 'She said she wasn't well enough. Pete Barton came but not her.'

'She missed my wedding to John. Same reason – she wasn't well.'

'She missed her own mother's funeral because she had a bad neck! She was over in Jersey the week Mum died but refused to stay for the funeral because she said she wanted to get back to the mainland to be fitted for a neck brace. The undertaker offered to get one for her but nothing would do but she left.'

'Ahh,' I said. 'That's why she wasn't on the list of mourners.' I explained about being shown that list by the funeral director when I went to Jersey with Eric in 1983. 'I don't think you were there either, were you?'

'It's very sad,' Sheila said. 'I was on holiday on the East Coast when Mum died, and when I got back there was a message that the police had been trying to contact me, but that was the day of the funeral so it was too late to get over to Jersey.'

'Oh, I'm sorry. What a shame!'

'Yes, it was. I went over to clear out the flat afterwards and Bernard gave me Daisy's phone number. We'd lost touch when I moved to Derbyshire with my first husband. I called her and gave her my new details. That's probably the last time I ever spoke to her.'

'But that was 1975! Do you mean you weren't in touch with her between then and her death in 1988?'

'No. I didn't even know she had died until the researcher from *Long Lost Family* told me. Life was pretty busy: I had three girls with my first husband then, after he died, I got remarried to Ivor and had Penny, so life was busy. To be honest, I didn't give Daisy a second thought until Penny rang me, saying that someone from *Long Lost Family* had been in touch, asking if I had a sister. You see, although she had given birth to me, Daisy had never been a fundamental part of my life. It's not as if I grew up in the same house as her.' She paused. 'How well did you get to know her?'

It was my turn to talk, and I told Sheila about my communication with Daisy and my meeting with the Barton children. 'They all seemed close,' I said. 'It's as if Daisy settled down in her thirties when she had her second family. They were a unit and I didn't ever feel I fitted into that.'

I showed her the glass bell Daisy had given me as a wedding present. 'It's pretty, but I'd far rather she had made the effort to come to the wedding.'

Sheila asked me about John and I pulled out some photographs to show her my extrovert, fun-loving second husband, describing his larger-than-life personality. 'We had over twenty great years together,' I said. 'It wasn't

237

nearly enough, but I'm learning to be grateful that I had him at all.'

'I was married to Ivor for forty years,' Sheila told me, and I could tell how much she loved him from the way she spoke and the soft expression in her eyes.

She showed me photographs of the three daughters I hadn't yet met: Susan Jane ('but we call her Jane'), Elizabeth and Julie, the girls from her first marriage who hadn't been able to make it to High Wycombe. They all looked lovely and I told her I hoped to meet them before too long.

'We'll have to arrange another reunion with all the extended family,' Sheila suggested.

'Oh, yes!' I sighed, already planning it in my imagination. 'Yes, let's.'

31

September in Spain

After Sheila left, I kept going over everything she'd told me and coming up with more questions for her. Fortunately, she was just on the end of a phone now.

'Where was Bellozanne Valley?' I called her to ask. 'I searched around when I was out there and no one had heard of it.'

'It's north-east of St Helier. I'm not surprised you didn't find it, because it's been turned into a rubbish tip and recycling plant now. It used to be pretty countryside when I was a girl.'

'Ah, that explains it! Thank you!'

Another time I rang and asked, 'Was Daisy really a trained nurse? She told me she was an SEAN, a State Enrolled Assistant Nurse.'

'Not to my knowledge,' Sheila replied. 'She worked as a carer in Southampton, but I don't think she was ever a nurse.'

I thought back to the very affectionate woman I had met on just two occasions and wondered what had made her tick. We all reinvent our pasts to a degree, but she had made some pretty extensive revisions. I assume it was because she wanted me to think well of her, but it was unnecessary because I would have liked her anyway. Had she come to believe her own stories? Both Sheila and Val condemned her strongly for the way she discarded her first family seemingly without a second thought, but I felt sympathy for her too. She'd had a difficult time during the war and had made some questionable decisions, but she made up for it with her second family, who all seemed close and loving.

In September I flew out to visit Pete and Val at their villa, about an hour's drive south of Alicante. It's set on a hillside, with a stunning view of the Mediterranean to the front and pine-covered hills behind. The décor is colourful, very Spanish in style, with beautiful vases of silk flowers in every room and lots of windows making it feel light and spacious. Their swimming pool is set in a walled garden with lovely statues and sculptures, and the whole place is just so comfortable that I took a big sigh, kicked my shoes off and relaxed as soon as I arrived. Of course, it helped that Pete had a gin and tonic in my hand before I could draw breath.

Val and I sat out in the early evening sunshine with our

drinks to continue the fragmented telephone conversations we'd been having about our mutual backgrounds.

'Do you know anything about why Daisy gave you up for adoption?' I asked her. 'With me, I think Henri Le Gresley Noël, our father, had left her for Lil the Welshwoman and she couldn't afford to be a single mum in wartime. She'd been staying with her sister, but got thrown out after insulting her husband. So I guess she didn't have much choice.'

'She obviously didn't have much money at the time, because I was born in a workhouse, Birch Hill House near Rochdale.'

'Really? I thought workhouses were Victorian institutions.'

'I've done some research into it and Birch Hill was built as a hospital for soldiers in the First World War then turned into a workhouse. A couple of years after I was born it reverted to a hospital again.'

'I suppose Daisy had just arrived on the boat from Jersey and had no money. When were you born?'

'End of July 1940.'

'That's only about a month after she was evacuated. Do you know if Henri Le Gresley was with her at the time?'

'I've got no idea. He was in the Royal Artillery so I expect he was off fighting. I don't think soldiers got compassionate leave to attend childbirth during wartime.'

'How long were you with Daisy before you were adopted?'

'Well, I know I was taken away from her when I was just nine days old. I heard a rumour that she'd had some kind of breakdown but there's no proof. Then there are five missing months before I was adopted by my mum and dad, Alexander James Anderson and Nora Anderson. They lived on Hayling Island near Portsmouth. I've done everything I can to find out where I was in those five months but not come up with anything.'

'I suppose you must have been in care of some kind.'

'I guess so. I don't know which agency arranged my adoption or anything more about the circumstances.' Val shrugged.

'Were they nice, your adoptive parents?'

'Oh yes, I had a wonderful childhood. My father was second to none, a fantastic man. As a child I spent a lot of time with him. He was very understanding, even when I got to my teens and went through a rebellious phase, as you do. And when my sons were born, he absolutely idolised them.'

'What was his job?'

'During the war he had been based in Portsmouth as a Royal Marine, then afterwards we moved to Kent, where he worked in the Royal Marine Police Armaments Depot.'

'You said in the *Long Lost Family* programme that all

this time you didn't even realise you were adopted. Why do you think your parents didn't tell you?'

'Goodness knows why. I don't think Mum wanted me to know and Dad just went along with it. It was swept under the carpet. Looking back, there were certain indications: I remember someone once referring to Mum as my stepmother, but I didn't think anything of it at the time.'

The sun was beginning to set behind the house, and the Mediterranean was darkening while the hills were glowing pink. We both paused to admire the view before we continued.

'How did you find out, then?' I asked.

'After Dad died I found an adoption certificate for me in a box of his papers.' She shook her head in disbelief. It was an incredible shock at the time. I genuinely didn't have a clue until I found that certificate.'

I felt very grateful to my own mum and dad for making me aware of my adoption from the start. It definitely made things easier. 'Did you ever think of trying to trace your birth mother and father? Didn't you wonder if you might have sisters somewhere?'

'I just assumed I was a mistake. I thought, "Don't go delving and open a can of worms." You never know what the future might have held for a mother and father who've given away a child.'

243

'Did you ever try to talk to your mum about it?'

'She wouldn't talk about anything. I'd ask her a question and she'd say, "No, no, I'm not talking about it." That was her stock answer.'

'Well, at least you had Pete by then.'

As if on cue, he came out to join us. 'Thought you girls might like a top-up,' he said, refreshing our drinks, then sitting down beside Val. They were lovely together. There was lots of witty verbal sparring but you could tell they were genuine soulmates.

'I know about Val's work,' I said, 'but what was your line of business, Pete?'

'I had a company doing building and house maintenance,' he said. 'I retired about ten years ago and we bought a holiday home out here in Spain, but once we had it we couldn't stay away. We liked it so much in this area that we started looking for a villa, then we came to live here for good in 2003.'

'I can see why,' I said. 'It's absolutely gorgeous.' The sun had set by now and a slick of white moonlight was shimmering on the distant ocean, like a magic pathway. Suddenly, there was a loud clicking sound like firecrackers and I jumped out of my skin. 'What on earth is that?'

'It's the cicadas,' Val explained, laughing at my reaction. 'They're flying beetles. Summer is their mating season, and when one starts making that clicking noise, they all start. There are loads of them in that derelict *finca* behind the house, which is surrounded by pine trees.'

We went inside for dinner and over the meal we talked of more recent events, but afterwards the conversation strayed back to our shared birth family and Val asked: 'You knew Daisy more recently than Sheila. Tell me honestly what you thought of her. What kind of person did she seem to you?'

'Honestly? I liked her. Call me soft, but I found her a friendly, outgoing character. I must show you the letters she sent me: she was very loving, on paper at least.'

'But now you know about all the lies, what do you think of her now?'

'I think she was a very complicated woman. I could try to make excuses for her and say she had it tough during the war years when our dad left her and so forth. Daisy obviously became a good mother to the Barton children, based on the little I saw of them together, and she must have convinced the council that she was adequate because she passed all the necessary tests to become a foster mother in her later years. But you, Sheila and me – the first family – definitely got the short straw.'

Despite what had transpired, I would always be glad I had known Daisy, albeit briefly. I wish I could have met my birth father, Henri Le Gresley Noël, as well. I wanted as much information as possible about where I came from. I wanted to tell my children and grandchildren what I had learned and instil in them a sense of our shared family history for them to pass down to future generations. It's part of what made us who we are.

32

Bonding by the Pool

As we lounged by the swimming pool the next day, in sunshine that was pleasantly warm without being scorching, I asked Val about what she thought when she first heard from the *Long Lost Family* team.

'I got a phone call one day from a lady saying she was calling on behalf of *Long Lost Family*. "Someone's trying to trace you," she said, and I said, "Really? Who?" And she said, "Did you know you've got a sister?" I said, "No!" And she said, "You also have a half-sister." Then she asked if I minded if *Long Lost Family* got in touch with me. I was absolutely gobsmacked, couldn't believe it, but I said yes straight away. So two days later Nicky Campbell arrived with a film crew and came in, and we sat at the table in the sun lounge to talk. He told me about Daisy leaving Sheila behind in Jersey and you and me being adopted,

247

and I was OK at that, but when he showed me your photos I had a little cry. The likeness was so amazing.'

'I remember you saying on camera that an only child is a lonely child. Is that how you felt growing up?'

Val nodded. 'I used to have friends who had brothers and sisters, and I always sort of envied them their family life. I had plenty of friends but when I got home there were no siblings to play with or talk to. You can tell I'm still in shock when you watch the TV programme. I just keep saying, "Two sisters? It's amazing!" or, "Isn't that amazing?" Everything's "amazing".'

'Yeah, I keep repeating the word "wonderful" in my clips,' I laughed. 'Were you at all nervous about being filmed?'

'Not at all,' she said. 'I'll tell you when I was nervous, though. The night before we all met in High Wycombe, I was up from three in the morning in a bit of a state. I said to Pete, "I can't do this, I want to go home." I think I was still in shock from finding out about you two. When I went down for breakfast, my son and granddaughter were there and Kerry said, "Come on, Nan, you've got to eat something." She got me a plate of food but I just pushed it around.'

'Who came to pick you up for the filming?'

'Nicky Campbell came to see how I was, but I'd calmed down a lot by then. They filmed me getting into the taxi

and I was still thinking, "Oh, I don't know about this …"
It was OK when we arrived – Danesfield House is such a
beautiful place – but the film crew told me to go down
some steps and take the first left, and I got lost in some
mixed conifer trees. "No, *second* left," the crew called, and
I walked out and saw you standing there.'

'Were you OK once we'd met and were all sitting down?
I was still a bit shaky then.'

'I thought it all went very well. We've got this amazing
resemblance, the same sort of hands. And then the dinner
at night was lovely. I've got no regrets at all.'

'My only regret is that we didn't meet earlier, and that
we didn't grow up together.'

Val laughed. 'If we'd grown up together we'd have had
our moments of scrapping, but we'd have stuck together
through thick and thin. Don't you agree?'

'Oh yes,' I said. I was glowing from the warmth of the
sun, but most of all from the amazing feeling of chatting
to my sister – one of my sisters. It was cosy and intimate,
everything I'd always hoped it would be like with a sibling.

I liked Pete a lot as well. He teased Val and sometimes
she cussed him from here to kingdom come, but you could
tell she loved him to pieces. It must have been an adjust-
ment for him, suddenly to have two sisters appearing on
his doorstep, but he took it in his stride and couldn't have
made me feel more welcome. As well as two sisters, I'd

gained a brother-in-law, and soon he was teasing me just as relentlessly as he teased everyone else.

'When are you going home, then?' he asked, with a grin. 'Do you realise I've had to miss my golf this week because of you?'

I liked his playful banter and tried to give as good as I got. 'Golf is an old man's game. Val and I are doing our best to keep you young.'

We had a wonderful week together, exploring the local area, going out for nice meals in restaurants and talking virtually non-stop. One evening, Val held what she called 'a gathering' so I could meet her local friends. About twenty folk came to enjoy a generously loaded buffet. Val made the most delicious pastry I'd ever tasted and a lemon cake made with lemons from the trees in their garden, which was divine. There were plentiful drinks – it *is* Spain, after all – and I genuinely liked all her friends out there.

Val and I chatted about Christmas coming and she asked if I had any plans. Graham and Helen were usually at their partners' families on Christmas Day, so I told her that I tended to see them and my grandchildren a week or so beforehand.

'I don't know what I'm doing this year,' I said. 'How about you?' And before I left we had agreed that I would go out to spend Christmas with them. I couldn't believe how generous they were to include me in their celebrations. I felt like crying. At long last it seemed as though I had the proper family I'd always yearned for.

33

Learning to Be Sisters in Our Seventies

When three women in their late sixties and early seventies meet for the first time and are told they are sisters, there's no guarantee they will even like each other. Lots of families who've grown up together drift apart in adult life, and sometimes communication breaks down, either because of a specific argument or just lack of effort, so what chance is there when you only meet for the first time later in life? I'd heard from the *Long Lost Family* team that a few people they have reunited over the years simply didn't find what they were looking for in each other and did not remain in touch, which seemed to me a terrible waste.

I had longed for a sister for such a long time that I was determined to make the relationships with Sheila and Val work out, no matter what. However, we were all three of us independent, feisty women who'd grown up as only children, which meant we didn't have any experience of how the sibling relationship worked. We'd all had close friendships in our life, of course, but we hadn't had the rough and tumble of shared childhoods, which teaches siblings about compromise and sharing and how to fight and make up again. It was inevitable that there would be a certain jostling for position as we found our places in the threesome. Fortunately, all three of us seemed to want to make things work, and not just me.

My Christmas with Val was wonderful. When I arrived, kicked my shoes off and curled up in her armchair, it felt like coming home. I glanced out the window to see something odd floating in the pool.

'What on earth is that?' I asked, and Val and Pete chuckled.

'It's a blow-up man. Our daughter-in-law sent it for Pete so he doesn't feel too outnumbered with two women in the house! We blew it up and sent it out for a swim!'

Things did get quite girly at times. Val and I put on mud face masks one day, and she took photos of us with our eyes staring out of the tightening black paste then put them up on Facebook. Half an hour later a message popped up: over in London, Graham had posted photos of two glamorous blondes underneath, with the caption 'Look how they turned out!'

My seventieth birthday loomed in early March 2013, and Val and Pete made my night by flying over for the party I held in a local Devon pub. I looked rather unusual that evening, and it was all because of my granddaughter Hannah.

'Do you think it would be all right if I wore purple nail varnish for the party?' I had asked her. I never normally looked after my nails, but it seemed I should do something special for the occasion.

'Nah, you're too old for purple,' she said, with the casual cruelty of youth.

That was a red rag to a bull, so not only did I get purple nails, but I had my hairdresser give me a purple fringe as well. (A few months later I got her to dye my grey hair blonde; I was determined not to turn into a 'grey old person', and decided to be forever sixty-nine. Decade birthdays have this effect on me: for my sixtieth I'd gone a deep dark brown with pillar-box red streaks, causing John to exclaim, 'What the hell have you done?' I'm still trying to decide what I'll do for eighty ...)

To find people who share my black, twisted sense of humour is quite rare, but Val, Pete and I laughed at the same things, and that birthday party was full of laughter. It was lovely to be able to show them my home, although they stayed in a hotel – where Val kept complaining about the cold. March in Devon tends to be a good ten to fifteen degrees colder than March in Alicante.

Straight afterwards, it was time for our second family reunion, which we'd organised to take place around the anniversary of our first meeting in High Wycombe. We chose a hotel in Folkestone and roped in as many family members as we could. I think there were around twenty of us who came along, and I met two more of Sheila's daughters, Jane and Elizabeth, and their families. We all had a meal in the hotel, but afterwards we couldn't find a place to sit in the bar because, unbeknownst to us when we booked, there was a rock 'n' roll weekend going on and the place was full of old rockers with their leather jackets and quiffs. I went to have a chat with the manager and he agreed to open an old nightclub for us downstairs, where we had plenty of space and could actually hear ourselves speak without fighting over the strains of Elvis, Bill Haley and the Rolling Stones.

That follow-up reunion was such a success that we decided to plan one for the following year. I was out in Spain with Val and Pete during the Christmas of 2013–14 – my second Christmas in a row with them – and we decided that we had to sort out the date for the reunion and book a hotel. We thought Sheila had already agreed to a particular date so we went ahead and made the booking, but when we told Sheila on Skype, she was furious with us.

'How dare you organise it without consulting me!' she raged, expressing her annoyance in quite strident terms.

'Well, that's the last time I ever arrange anything,' Val exploded, and she strode off to sit on the settee, leaving me on my own in front of the computer.

I tried to smooth the waters, but at one point I glanced round to see what Val was doing and Sheila snapped at me, 'Don't look at her like that!'

It was our first disagreement and I was upset about it at the time – but when we next Skyped Sheila it was as if nothing had happened. I realised that both Val and Sheila are the kind of women who don't hold back their feelings. They can blow up, but five minutes later it's all forgotten. I'm not like that. I hardly ever blow up. If someone is cross with me, I retreat into silence, which can sometimes have the unfortunate effect of making them even crosser. If at all possible, I prefer to avoid conflict, but I could see that wasn't going to be possible all the time with two sisters with such strong personalities.

'Now we know each other, the occasional little disagreement doesn't hurt, does it?' Val said.

It was a lesson I had to learn: not to be upset if one or other of them was sharp with me on occasion, and to try to express my own feelings instead of closing up like a clam. Getting things out in the open is always healthier than bottling them up; I could see that logically, but it just took practice to learn to do it.

I also realised that the three of us had quite different styles when it came to making arrangements: I tend to do everything with a broad brush and work out the details later; Val is a good planner and great at doing the paperwork; while Sheila is a details person and likes to nail down every last item. We found our way of working together with a bit of trial and error along the way.

A hotel in Thurrock, Essex, was booked for our March 2014 reunion, and just as we were fine-tuning the details, I had a phone call from a girl on the *Long Lost Family* team, asking if we'd be interested in taking part in a follow-up programme to see how we were all getting along with each other.

'Funny you should say that …' I said, and explained about the forthcoming reunion.

'Perfect!' she said. 'We'll come along and film you there.'

It was a different film crew from the one I'd worked with back in 2012, but equally as friendly and professional. The day before Val arrived they took Sheila and me to an old manor house, where they interviewed us individually about how we felt about our new sisters.

'When we met, it was, "Oh my God, can I do this?"' I explained on camera. 'I've never been somebody's sister.

I'd always wanted a brother or sister to feel that very strong connection, so when we first met I was physically, emotionally and mentally overwhelmed ... but now there's an excitement in life again. I look forward to every day because I've found out who I am: I'm part of a trio. I've always had to stand on my own and now I don't. I hope I live long enough to really enjoy it. I just want to go forward as a family – that is so lovely.'

In Sheila's interview she spoke about how much she likes using the words 'my sister'. 'I tell people, "I can't do anything on Sunday night because I'm Skyping *my sister*." Just to be able to say "my sister" is really lovely.'

Sheila and I went shopping in the Lakeside Shopping Centre then had dinner on our own that evening, and it was lovely to spend the time together and catch up on everything, since I'd seen more of Val than I had of her during the year. Pete and Val arrived the following morning, and the *Long Lost Family* team whisked us off to another of the fabulous locations they have a knack of finding, this time a café in Leigh-on-Sea. I'd never been there before but the name rang a bell because John used to meet his mates at a pub called The Peter Boat along the front there. We passed the very place, and it was nice to think of him sitting there on a sunny summer's afternoon, no doubt entertaining his mates with some risqué anecdote or other, told loudly, with a gin and tonic or a pint in his hand.

Val, Sheila and I walked along the seafront and sat down to be filmed in a lovely little dog-walkers' café, which was basically a glorified hut with beautiful décor. The outside space was full of dogs and their owners, and rugs and hot-water bottles were handed out to anyone who was feeling the chill. There was a view out to sea, and it was every bit as nice a day as the one two years earlier when we all met in High Wycombe. The March sun was bright, if not particularly warm, and there was a clear blue sky above.

The team asked us to chat about our relationship now and Sheila began: 'We've got big sis, middle sis and baby sis, and I'm the big one.'

'There's definitely, definitely a connection between us now,' Val said.

We all agreed that it was odd getting used to being a sister in our seventies, but Sheila said, 'This is fulfilling my bucket list, us sitting here having a cup of coffee. It's something I've always wanted to do.'

We had brought photographs of ourselves back in the 1980s, at the time when we could have met if only Daisy had told me about my sisters. Sheila looked very pretty in a white dress with dark-brown shortish hair; Val was resplendent in a bright-blue evening dress with shoulder pads and shoulder-length curly blonde hair; and I looked like one of the Bay City Rollers in my feather-cut hairstyle and a big white jumper. Our fashion sense was completely different but we all had the same mouth, with the same smile, which was obvious when we put the photos on the table alongside each other. You could truly see that we were related.

'Oh, to be that age and know what we know now,' I sighed. 'I'll have to live to be a hundred. There's too much to fit in.' If only I had met Sheila and Val back in the eighties: we could have been there for each other when John and Ivor passed away; we could have helped when Pete and Val retired and went to live in Spain; we could have celebrated our children's significant landmarks and the births of our grandchildren. Still, there's no sense in looking backwards. The important thing is to cherish what we have now.

The *Long Lost Family* team filmed us walking along the front then shot a little of the family reunion at the hotel that evening, before leaving us to get on with it. Once again, I looked round at all the smiling faces and had to pinch myself: these people were members of my family. Two years on, I still hadn't quite got used to the idea. It's still new and I'm still learning.

It's just lovely to be able to pick up the phone if there's a problem or you've got something on your mind. Val has a number to call her in Spain and only be charged local rates, so I'm on the phone to her virtually every day. I speak to Sheila less often – she moans that she can never catch me because I'm always out and about with the horses, the dogs or the old folks – but we never let too much time go by.

One evening, Helen was over and telling me about a problem her son Joe was having at school when I suddenly found I had tears in my eyes. I wiped them away, saying, 'Silly me, what am I on about?'

'You've changed, Mum,' Helen said thoughtfully. 'You're much more emotional than you used to be.'

'Really?'

'Yes, really. You must have noticed. At first I was a bit like, "Whoa, what's happening?" but I'm getting used to it now.'

I stared at her. Could it be true? Me, the woman who had always been scared of strong emotions, who bottled things up and dealt with practicalities instead: could I be getting soft in my old age? When I began to think about it, I remembered that I had surprised myself by getting tears in my eyes over an item on the news the night before. Maybe Helen had a point.

'I always felt that I was too reserved and unemotional as a mother to you and Graham. You had everything you wanted materially and physically, but I wasn't as loving as I could have been.'

'Hmm … we weren't a very huggy family, were we? Yet look at you now – you hug blooming everyone!'

Yes, it was true. I had become one of life's huggers. I hug everybody these days.

'It was meeting your sisters that changed you,' Helen said bluntly. 'It's good. It means you're not hiding your feelings any more. You're more open. More approachable.'

After she left, I thought about what she'd said. I got out the DVD of the first *Long Lost Family* programme I took part in and watched it again, and I could almost see myself learning to express emotions during the course of the show. At the beginning, I'm very matter-of-fact and almost cold, as I relate the story of my childhood and my search for Sheila without any emotion. But after meeting Sheila and Val, I'm bubbling over with excitement, and by the reunion programme I'm frequently wiping away tears and clearly being emotional and honest about my feelings.

It's as if the little nine-year-old girl who was told not to cry when her mummy died has at last learned not to be afraid of strong emotion. I can let my feelings out and simply be myself. It may have taken me till the age of seventy-two to discover this, but better late than never. And I owe it all to my wonderful new-found sisters. In more ways than they know, they've made my life complete.

Acknowledgements

First of all, my heartfelt thanks to Gill Paul for her patience and skill, without which this book would never have happened. She found all this order among the chaos of my thoughts.

Also to all at *Long Lost Family*, especially Ella Bahaire and Louise Palmer. They guided me through this life-changing time with unimaginable empathy, gentleness and kindness, hand in hand with professionalism.

To Kate Latham, my editor at HarperCollins, for making the book happen. Thank you for all your help and encouragement.

And, of course, my sisters Sheila and Val: how they coped with me crash-landing in their lives never ceases to amaze me. Together, we are working through the next phase of our lives, three women raised as only children now learning what sisters are. Love you, girls!